Mini DONUTS

100
Bite-Sized
DONUT RECIPES
— TO —
Sweeten Your
"Hole" Day

Mini
DONUTS

Jessica Segarra
Creator of *The Novice Chef* Blog

Published by
Adams Media, a division of F+W Media, Inc.
57 Littlefield Street, Avon, MA 02322. U.S.A.
www.adamsmedia.com

ISBN 10: 1-4405-4341-0
ISBN 13: 978-1-4405-4341-8
eISBN 10: 1-4405-4342-9
eISBN 13: 978-1-4405-4342-5

Printed in the United States of America.

10   9   8   7   6   5   4   3

Always follow safety and commonsense cooking protocol while using
kitchen utensils, operating ovens and stoves, and handling uncooked
food. If children are assisting in the preparation of any recipe, they
should always be supervised by an adult.

Many of the designations used by manufacturers and sellers to distinguish
their product are claimed as trademarks. Where those designations
appear in this book and Adams Media was aware of a trademark claim,
the designations have been printed with initial capital letters.

Photos courtesy of Jessica Segarra.
Donut icon © 123RF.com

This book is available at quantity discounts for bulk purchases.
For information, please call 1-800-289-0963.

I am dedicating this book to a smart woman who used to hide donuts under her bed. The apple sure doesn't fall far from the tree. I love you, Mama!

Acknowledgments

First and foremost, I have to thank my husband, Jorge. Thank you for eating 505 bajillion donuts and never complaining when we had donuts for breakfast, lunch, and dinner. I simply cannot thank you enough for your endless taste-testing, your honest critiques, and your endless help with the dishes.

Also, a ginormous thanks to my wonderful editor, Ross, and everyone else behind the scenes at Adams Media. Thank you for holding my hand through this whole process. Writing my first cookbook was scary, but you made it a great experience!

And last, but certainly not least, thank you to my wonderful friends and family. Sure, I could name names, but we would be here all day. Thank you for your love and support and offers to help eat donuts!

Contents

Chapter 5 BAKERY SPECIALS 95

Chapter 6 CANDY-AISLE DONUTS 113

Chapter 7 DRINKS TO DONUTS 131

Chapter 8 FOR THE KID IN YOU 149

Introduction

If you're a donut lover—and since you have this book in your hands, you must be—that neon "Hot Now" sign in the window of a donut shop makes you weak in the knees. A tender, fluffy donut dripping in clear, warm glaze is enough to send anyone pulling into that drive-through lane, but now you can have that same glorious experience in your own kitchen.

With just a handful of kitchen staples, a whisk, and a few multicolored sprinkles, you are well on your way to filling your stomach with tons of divine donuts. Instead of traditional-sized donuts, this cookbook focuses on smaller, more adorable mini donuts. Sure, they are as delicious and comforting as their bigger cousins, but their two-bite size makes them that much more fun—and a little more waistline-friendly!

Now, when you think of mini donuts, you may only think of breakfast. Of course, breakfast and donuts go hand in hand, but these little darlings also make the perfect dessert. Imagine walking into a dinner party and seeing the dessert table filled with towers of brightly colored, tender, mouthwatering bite-sized donuts. It's a childhood dream come true! Or instead of a dinner party, how about throwing a donut-decorating party, where everyone can make their own adorable party favors. Fill a table with already-baked donuts, your favorite frostings, a variety of sprinkles, and a bunch of chopped-up candy bars . . . and yours will be the most talked-about party for weeks.

Whether you're looking for an old-fashioned favorite, like the Cinnamon-Sugar Mini Donut; a sweet-savory combo, like the Chocolate-Bacon-Maple Mini Donut; or a fruity bite of Lemon Meringue Mini Donut, you can't go wrong. So turn the page, pick out a recipe, and get ready to put a big smile on your face. It's time to get this donut party started. Enjoy!

Part 1
MINI DONUTS 101

Blueberry Cake Mini Donuts
(Chapter 1)

Like you, I am and will always be a home cook and baker. I don't use crazy kitchen tools, extremely rare ingredients, or difficult techniques—which means that all the recipes found in *Mini Donuts* are approachable and easily achieved. All you have to do to make your own amazing mini donuts is give the recipes a try!

In keeping with this mindset, when developing these recipes, I tried to keep the busy woman in the back of my mind. Would she have cake flour? No, but she likely has regular, all-purpose flour. Would she have a specialty creamed honey? Probably not, but a big jar of local honey might be sitting in her cupboard. Is a fancy fruit, in season for only two weeks of the year, ripening on her counter? Probably not. The ingredients used in the following recipes are regular, everyday staples in most kitchens. If you don't have something, it can be easily found in your local grocery store—or, in some cases, your local liquor store. In addition, none of the ingredients costs an arm and a leg!

That said, there are a few items that you want to be familiar with before you start your mini-donut journey.

EQUIPMENT AND SUPPLIES

You don't need to have a kitchen filled with every fancy culinary toy on the market to successfully recreate these recipes. In fact, all you really need are the following:

- Baking racks
- Deep fryer
- Mini-donut machine or mini-donut pan
- Piping bag and round tip
- Sifter
- Stand mixer
- Wax paper

All of these items will increase your success of making perfect mini-donuts, every single time!

METHODS OF MAKING MINI DONUTS

The recipes in this cookbook use three different methods of cooking mini donuts: the donut pan, the mini-donut machine, and the frying method. Each method gives your mini donut a different type of texture.

- The donut pan produces a mini donut with a light, airy, cupcake-like texture.
- The mini-donut machine creates a more dense, cakelike donut with a perfectly rounded top.
- The frying method, either in a deep fryer or a deep pan with hot oil, creates a donut very similar to those you most often find in a donut shop.

It's important to keep in mind that each of these methods uses different preparation techniques, as discussed below. Try them all to find which texture and technique you like best.

Donut-Pan Method

When baking mini donuts in your donut pan, there are a few things to keep in mind:

- **Grease it.** Greasing your mini-donut pan is imperative. There are a great number of ways to grease it, but the best ways are to grease the pan with butter, with the aerosol spray Baker's Joy, or with a napkin and a little vegetable oil.
- **Overfilling is a crime.** Do not overfill the mini-donut indentations with batter. When they are overfilled, the donuts tend to bake up over the edges and grow out instead of up, giving you flat mini "mushrooms."
- **Know your oven.** If your oven tends to get hotter on one side, be sure to rotate the donut pan halfway through the baking time. On the other hand, if your oven usually takes a little longer to bake than the time a recipe calls for, bump up the heat by 10°F to make up for it.

Mini Donut–Machine Method

When baking donuts in your mini-donut machine, there are a few things to keep in mind:

- **Know your nonstick.** Most of the mini-donut machines are nonstick. If yours isn't—or if your donuts are sticking—spray a little Baker's Joy on it before each round of donuts are baked.
- **Work fast.** Because of the high heat, getting the batter into all six donut indentations swiftly is imperative. To do this, pipe the batter in with a piping bag or Ziploc bag with the tip cut off the

end. Otherwise, the donuts begin to cook before you are ready to close the lid, and they tend to bake over the edges while you are trying to fill the rest of the indentions.

- **Flip it.** Most donut machines do not cook as evenly as you would like: one side of the donut is usually a little harder than the other. To help offset that issue, flip the donut halfway through baking, using a toothpick or the two-pronged fork included with your machine.
- **Don't overbake.** Unless you like your donuts as dry as the Sahara Desert, watch them carefully. Donut machines provide an incredible amount of heat, and they really do cook the mini donuts in 3 to 4 minutes. Keep an eye on them, and remove donuts promptly to prevent overbaking.

The Frying Method

When frying mini donuts, there are a few helpful tips to keep in mind:

- **Stay safe.** While the oil doesn't look dangerous, as soon as you drop in the first ball of dough, watch out! The oil will easily pop and burn you if you are not cautious. To help avoid any injury, use a long-handled slotted spoon to both drop in and remove mini donuts.
- **Watch the heat.** When frying anything, it is extremely easy to let the temperature creep up on you. Keep an eye on the thermometer to ensure that the oil remains at the correct temperature (the temperature varies by donut, so check each recipe for details). Just a few degrees higher than

needed and you will wind up with burned mini donuts.

- **Keep it light.** Nobody likes to bite into a donut and find that it's full of grease. To avoid this faux pas, be sure to shake the donut as it comes out of the fryer to remove any excess oil. Then, place the donut on a plate lined with paper towels or newspaper to soak up any remaining grease. If needed, after allowing donuts to rest for a minute or two, flip them to drain the other side.

TIME TO MAKE THE DONUTS!

Baking delicious mini donuts should be fun, easy, and accessible—and these qualities are exactly what you'll find in the recipes in Part 2. Take your time, and read through the entire recipe before you start; knowing what's ahead helps you to prepare yourself mentally, as well as your ingredients and your equipment. So grab your apron! It's time to make the donuts!

Part 2

THE RECIPES

White Chocolate–Red Velvet Mini Donuts (Chapter 2)

*T*here are few things in this world as tantalizing as a plain, hot, glazed donut, but you'll be happily surprised at the multitude of flavor options found in the recipes in this part. Here, you will find recipes ranging from Orange Soda to Salted Caramel to Banana Cream, and even a chocolate S'mores Mini Donut. It doesn't matter if you are a lover of chocolate, a salty-sweet fan, or a plain-Jane kind of girl. Whatever you like, this part has you covered!

Chapter 1

THE CLASSICS

You can't have a cookbook about mini donuts without starting with the classics. While you may typically be the first one in line for a fancy S'mores Mini Donut (Chapter 8), sometimes you just need a warm Cinnamon-Sugar Mini Donut that melts in your mouth, or a brightly speckled Vanilla-Sprinkle Mini Donut. With its burst of colored sprinkles and crisp vanilla flavor, it is always one of the first to go. When you are looking for comfort and familiarity, you just have to whip up a batch of the favorites found in this chapter. They're guaranteed to hit the spot every single time!

Glazed Fried Mini Donut

YIELDS 26 MINI DONUTS AND
26 MINI DONUT HOLES

FOR DONUTS

2 tablespoons water, warmed

1.25-ounce envelope fast-rise yeast

¾ cup whole milk, warmed

¼ cup granulated sugar

½ teaspoon salt

1 large egg

3 tablespoons shortening or lard

2½ cups all-purpose flour

Vegetable oil or peanut oil, for frying

FOR GLAZE

2 tablespoons whole milk

1 teaspoon vanilla extract

1½ cups powdered sugar

....

FAST-RISE YEAST

If you can't find fast-rise yeast or you already have regular yeast, don't worry! You can easily use regular yeast in its place. Fast-rise yeast does exactly what it says: makes the donuts rise faster. If you use regular yeast, just expect a little longer rise time.

Nothing can beat the nostalgic taste of a hot, fresh, glazed donut. You can try, but the fluffy texture and warm glaze make this donut one of the best classics around. Whip out your deep fryer, and see if you can resist!

1. In the bowl of your stand mixer, with the paddle attachment (or in a large bowl if you are going to knead the dough by hand), mix together warm water and yeast and let stand for 5 minutes.
2. Add milk, sugar, salt, egg, shortening, and 1 cup of flour. Mix on medium-low for 2 minutes, then switch to the dough hook. Slowly add the remaining 1½ cups of flour, ½ cup at a time. Once you have added all the flour, knead on medium for 2–3 minutes, until dough no longer sticks to the bowl. Turn up the speed to medium-high, and continue to knead dough for 3–4 minutes, until dough is smooth.
3. Transfer dough to a greased bowl, and cover with a slightly damp tea towel. Place bowl in a warm area (or in an oven preheated to 200°F and then turned off) for about 1 hour. Dough is ready when it has doubled in size.
4. Transfer raised dough to a lightly floured surface, and carefully roll out until it is ½" thick. Cut out donuts with a floured 2" biscuit cutter, and then cut out the center of each donut with a floured 1" biscuit cutter.
5. Place donuts and donut holes on a lightly floured cookie sheet, and cover again with a slightly damp tea towel. Place in a warm area (or in an oven preheated to 200°F and then turned off) for about 1 hour. Dough is ready when it has doubled in size.
6. Heat oil in a large, deep skillet or a deep fryer to 350°F.
7. Once oil is hot, working with 4 to 6 donuts at a time, carefully drop donuts into oil. Fry for 1–2 minutes or until golden brown; flip each donut and fry the other side.
8. Remove and drain on a plate lined with paper towels or newspaper. Continue this process until each donut has been fried.
9. Place wax paper under a wire rack to collect any drippings for an easy cleanup. Then, in a small bowl, whisk together milk and vanilla extract. Add powdered sugar, whisking until smooth.
10. While the donuts are still warm, dip the top of each donut and donut hole into the glaze, transfer to a wire rack, and let set for 5 minutes. Serve immediately; donuts can be stored in an airtight container for up to 3 days but are best served fresh.

Glazed Fried Mini Donuts

Cinnamon-Sugar Mini Donut

 YIELDS 30 MINI DONUTS

FOR DONUTS

1⅓ cups all-purpose flour, sifted

2 teaspoons baking powder

½ teaspoon ground cinnamon

¼ teaspoon salt

1 large egg

½ cup granulated sugar

¾ cup whole milk

3 tablespoons vegetable oil

2 teaspoons vanilla extract

FOR TOPPING

2 teaspoons ground cinnamon

½ cup granulated sugar

3 tablespoons butter, melted

Found everywhere from donut shops to gas-station shelves (and now in your kitchen), the Cinnamon-Sugar donut is a true classic. It's probably the easiest of all the donuts to make, but that doesn't mean it isn't one of the best tasting. This classic doesn't have to be fancy to be delicious!

1. If using an electric donut maker, preheat according to manufacturer's instructions. If using donut pans, preheat oven to 350°F and grease donut pans.
2. In a small bowl, sift together flour, baking powder, cinnamon, and salt. Set aside.
3. In a medium bowl, whisk together egg and sugar, then add milk, oil, and vanilla extract, mixing until thoroughly combined. Gently stir in the flour mixture, stirring until there are no lumps.
4. **If using mini-donut pans:** Carefully fill each donut indentation ¾ full. Bake for 7–9 minutes or until a toothpick inserted into a donut comes out clean. Remove donuts from pan and transfer to a cooling rack. **If using an electric mini-donut maker:** Carefully fill each donut indentation ¾ full. Bake according to manufacturer's instructions or until a toothpick inserted into a donut comes out clean. Remove donuts from appliance, and transfer to a cooling rack.
5. Toss together cinnamon and sugar in a shallow bowl. While donuts are still hot, quickly dip them in melted butter and coat with the cinnamon-sugar mixture. Donuts are best when warm, and they do not store well, so serve immediately.

Cinnamon-Sugar Mini Donuts

Sour Cream Cake Fried Mini Donut

YIELDS 18 MINI DONUTS AND
18 MINI DONUT HOLES

FOR DONUTS

1 cup plus 2 tablespoons all-purpose flour

1 teaspoon baking powder

¼ teaspoon cinnamon

¼ teaspoon nutmeg

½ teaspoon salt

1 tablespoon shortening or lard

¼ cup sugar

1 large egg yolk

⅓ cup sour cream

Vegetable oil or peanut oil, for frying

FOR GLAZE

2 tablespoons whole milk

1 teaspoon vanilla extract

1½ cups powdered sugar

The sour cream in these mini donuts adds a tangy flavor and also keeps them incredibly moist, but the real secret to success is the double flip while frying. The double flip is the cause for all of the beautiful grooves and ridges on top of these mini-donuts!

1. In medium bowl, sift together flour, baking powder, cinnamon, nutmeg, and salt. Set aside.
2. In a large bowl or a stand mixer, cream together shortening and sugar. Add egg yolk and beat for 30 seconds, scraping down the bowl as needed. Then, alternating flour mixture and sour cream, combine all ingredients until just blended. Transfer batter into a clean bowl, cover with plastic wrap, and refrigerate for 1 hour (or maximum 24 hours).
3. Heat oil in a large, deep skillet or a deep fryer to 325°F.
4. While oil is heating up, transfer dough to a lightly floured surface, and carefully roll out until it is ½" thick. Cut out donuts with a floured 2" biscuit cutter, and then cut out the center of each donut with a floured 1" biscuit cutter.
5. Once oil is hot, working with 4 to 6 donuts at a time, carefully drop donuts into oil. Once donuts rise to the top, flip each donut and fry the other side for 1–1½ minutes or until golden brown. Then, flip donuts back to the first side, and fry for 1 additional minute or until golden brown.
6. Remove and drain on a plate lined with paper towels or newspaper. Continue this process until each donut has been fried.
7. Place wax paper under a wire rack to collect any drippings for an easy cleanup. Then, in a small bowl, whisk together milk and vanilla extract. Add powdered sugar, whisking until smooth.
8. While the donuts are still warm, dip the top of each donut and donut hole into the glaze, transfer to a wire rack, and let set for 5 minutes. Serve immediately, or store in an airtight container for up to 3 days.

Sour Cream Baked Mini Donut

 YIELDS 28 MINI DONUTS

FOR DONUTS

2 cups all-purpose flour, sifted

2 teaspoons baking powder

½ teaspoon cinnamon

¼ teaspoon salt

1 large egg

½ cup granulated sugar

¼ cup sour cream

2 tablespoons vegetable oil

1 teaspoon vanilla extract

¾ cup buttermilk

FOR ICING

1 tablespoon whole milk

1 teaspoon vanilla extract

1½ cups powdered sugar

Sour cream donuts are a staple in the donut world, and these mini donuts live up to the hype. Even though they're small, the creamy, tangy flavor of the sour cream and buttermilk helps these mini donuts pack a big taste!

1. If using an electric donut maker, preheat according to manufacturer's instructions. If using donut pans, preheat oven to 350°F and grease donut pans.
2. In a small bowl, sift together flour, baking powder, cinnamon, and salt. Set aside.
3. In a medium bowl, whisk together egg and sugar. Then, add sour cream, oil, and vanilla extract, mixing until thoroughly combined. Gently whisk in the flour mixture, alternating with the buttermilk, until there are no lumps. Transfer batter to a piping bag, or to a Ziploc bag with a hole cut in the tip.
4. **If using mini-donut pans:** Carefully fill each donut indentation ¾ full. Bake for 7–9 minutes or until a toothpick inserted into a donut comes out clean. Transfer donuts to a cooling rack and cool completely. **If using an electric mini-donut maker:** Carefully fill each donut indentation ¾ full. Bake according to manufacturer's instructions or until a toothpick inserted into a donut comes out clean. Remove donuts from appliance, transfer to a cooling rack, and let cool completely.
5. Place wax paper under a wire rack to collect any drippings for an easy cleanup. Then, in a small bowl, whisk together milk and vanilla extract. Add powdered sugar, whisking until smooth.
6. Dip the top of each donut into the icing, transfer to a wire rack, and let set for 5 minutes. Serve immediately; donuts can be stored in an airtight container for up to 3 days but are best served fresh.

Buttermilk Mini Donut

 YIELDS 28 MINI DONUTS

FOR DONUTS

1⅓ cups all-purpose flour, sifted

2 teaspoons baking powder

½ teaspoon ground cinnamon

¼ teaspoon nutmeg

¼ teaspoon salt

1 large egg

½ cup granulated sugar

½ cup sour cream

¼ cup vegetable oil

1 teaspoon vanilla extract

¾ cup buttermilk

FOR ICING

2 tablespoons buttermilk

1 teaspoon vanilla extract

1½ cups powdered sugar

Buttermilk donuts are famous for their sweet, tangy flavor and dense texture. The addition of sour cream helps to enhance the tangy quality, but the buttermilk is still the shining star in these mini masterpieces!

1. If using an electric donut maker, preheat according to manufacturer's instructions. If using donut pans, preheat oven to 350°F and grease donut pans.
2. In a small bowl, sift together flour, baking powder, cinnamon, nutmeg, and salt. Set aside.
3. In a medium bowl, whisk together egg and sugar. Then, add sour cream, oil, and vanilla extract, mixing until thoroughly combined. Gently stir in the flour mixture, alternating with the buttermilk, stirring until there are no large lumps.
4. **If using mini-donut pans:** Carefully fill each donut indentation ¾ full. Bake for 7–9 minutes or until a toothpick inserted into a donut comes out clean. Transfer donuts to a cooling rack and let cool completely. **If using an electric mini-donut maker:** Carefully fill each donut indentation ¾ full. Bake according to manufacturer's instructions or until a toothpick inserted into a donut comes out clean. Remove donuts from appliance, transfer to a cooling rack, and let cool completely.
5. Place wax paper under a wire rack to collect any drippings for an easy cleanup. Then, in a small bowl, whisk together buttermilk and vanilla extract. Add powdered sugar, whisking until smooth.
6. Dip the top of each donut into the icing, transfer to a wire rack, and let set for 5 minutes. Serve immediately; donuts can be stored in an airtight container for up to 3 days but are best served fresh.

USE THE REAL STUFF

With most baking recipes, it is okay to substitute a small amount of buttermilk with homemade buttermilk (lemon or vinegar and whole milk). But for this recipe, always use the real stuff. When the star is the buttermilk, you don't want to use a substitute.

Buttermilk Mini Donuts

Chocolate-Sour Cream Baked Mini Donut

 YIELDS 28 MINI DONUTS

FOR DONUTS

1⅔ cups all-purpose flour, sifted

⅓ cup cocoa powder, sifted

2 teaspoons baking powder

½ teaspoon cinnamon

¼ teaspoon salt

1 large egg

½ cup granulated sugar

¼ cup sour cream

2 tablespoons vegetable oil

1 teaspoon vanilla extract

¾ cup buttermilk

FOR ICING

1 tablespoon whole milk

1 teaspoon vanilla extract

1½ cups powdered sugar

When you add chocolate to a sour cream donut, you pretty much guarantee that your taste buds will be treated to a moist, sweet, chocolate treat. With a sprinkle of cinnamon, you are also deepening the chocolate flavor and giving the donut a spicy surprise!

1. If using an electric donut maker, preheat according to manufacturer's instructions. If using donut pans, preheat oven to 350°F and grease donut pans.
2. In a small bowl, sift together flour, cocoa powder, baking powder, cinnamon, and salt. Set aside.
3. In a medium bowl, whisk together egg and sugar. Then, add sour cream, oil, and vanilla extract, mixing until thoroughly combined. Gently whisk in the flour mixture, alternating with the buttermilk, until there are no lumps. Transfer batter to a piping bag, or to a Ziploc baggie with a hole cut in the tip.
4. **If using mini-donut pans:** Carefully fill each donut indentation ¾ full. Bake for 7–9 minutes or until a toothpick inserted into a donut comes out clean. Transfer donuts to a cooling rack and cool completely. **If using an electric mini-donut maker:** Carefully fill each donut indentation ¾ full. Bake according to manufacturer's instructions or until a toothpick inserted into a donut comes out clean. Remove donuts from appliance, transfer to a cooling rack, and let cool completely.
5. Place wax paper under a wire rack to collect any drippings for an easy cleanup. Then, in a small bowl, whisk together milk and vanilla extract. Add powdered sugar, whisking until smooth.
6. Dip the top of each donut into the icing, transfer to a wire rack, and let set for 5 minutes. Serve immediately; donuts can be stored in an airtight container for up to 3 days but are best served fresh.

Canned-Biscuit Fried Mini Donut

 YIELDS 24 MINI DONUTS

FOR DONUTS

Vegetable oil or peanut oil, for frying

1 16.3-ounce can of homestyle biscuits

FOR TOPPING

½ cup granulated sugar

2 teaspoons ground cinnamon

Some mornings it's nice to have hot donuts with minimal work in the kitchen. On those days, these Canned-Biscuit Fried Mini Donuts are the answer to your prayers. They're easy, fast, and delicious! What more could you want?

1. Heat oil in a large, deep skillet or a deep fryer to 350°F.
2. While oil is heating up, slice each biscuit into quarters. Toss together sugar and cinnamon in a shallow bowl and set aside.
3. Once oil is hot, working with 6 to 8 donuts at a time, carefully drop donuts into oil. Fry for 1–2 minutes or until golden brown; flip each donut and fry the other side.
4. Remove and drain on a plate lined with newspaper or paper towels. Continue working until each donut has been fried.
5. While donuts are still hot, quickly toss mini donuts in the cinnamon-sugar mixture. Donuts are best when still warm, and they do not store well, so serve immediately.

Jam-Filled Fried Mini Donut

 YIELDS 26 MINI DONUTS

A warm, fresh donut, coated with a sweet, sticky glaze and filled with jam, is pure sugar heaven. It only takes one more step to turn regular donuts into these darling Jam-Filled Fried Mini Donuts, so what are you waiting for? Take the time to turn your mini donuts into a classic!

FOR DONUTS

2 tablespoons water, warmed

1.25-ounce envelope fast rise yeast

¾ cup whole milk, warmed

¼ cup granulated sugar

½ teaspoon salt

1 large egg

3 tablespoons shortening or lard

2½ cups all-purpose flour

Vegetable oil or peanut oil, for frying

FOR FILLING

¾ cup of your favorite jam or jelly

FOR ICING

2 tablespoons whole milk

1 teaspoon vanilla extract

1½ cups powdered sugar

1. In the bowl of your stand mixer, with the paddle attachment (or in a large bowl if you are going to knead the dough by hand), whisk together warm water and yeast and let stand for 5 minutes.
2. Add milk, sugar, salt, egg, shortening, and 1 cup of flour. Mix on medium-low for 2 minutes, then switch to the dough hook. Slowly add the remaining 1½ cups flour, ½ cup at a time. Once you have added all the flour, knead on medium for 2–3 minutes, until dough no longer sticks to the bowl. Turn up the speed to medium-high, and continue to knead dough for 3–4 minutes, until dough is smooth.
3. Transfer dough to a greased bowl, and cover with a slightly damp tea towel. Place bowl in a warm area (or in an oven preheated to 200°F and then turned off) for about 1 hour. Dough is ready when it has doubled in size.
4. Transfer raised dough to a lightly floured surface, and carefully roll out until it is ½" thick. Cut out donuts with a floured 2" biscuit cutter.
5. Place donuts on a lightly floured cookie sheet, and cover again with a slightly damp tea towel. Place in a warm area (or in an oven preheated to 200°F and then turned off) for about 1 hour. Dough is ready when it has doubled in size.
6. Heat oil in a large, deep skillet or a deep fryer to 350°F.
7. Once oil is hot, working with 4 to 6 donuts at a time, carefully drop donuts into oil. Fry for 1–2 minutes or until golden brown; flip each donut and fry the other side.
8. Remove and drain on a plate lined with newspaper or paper towels. Continue this process until each donut has been fried.
9. Place wax paper under a wire rack to collect any drippings for an easy cleanup. Add jelly to a pastry bag fitted with a long, plain tip. Using the tip as a probe, fill the center of each mini donut with about 2 teaspoons of jelly. Transfer to a wire rack.
10. Then, in a small bowl, whisk together milk and vanilla extract. Add powdered sugar, whisking until smooth.
11. While the donuts are still warm, dip the top of each donut into the icing, transfer to a wire rack, and let set for 5 minutes. Serve immediately; donuts can be stored in an airtight container for up to 3 days but are best served fresh.

Maple-Glazed Mini Donut

 YIELDS 30 MINI DONUTS

FOR DONUTS

1⅓ cups all-purpose flour, sifted

2 teaspoons baking powder

¼ teaspoon salt

1 large egg

½ cup granulated sugar

¾ cup whole milk

3 tablespoons vegetable oil

2 teaspoons vanilla extract

FOR FROSTING

½ teaspoon whole milk

2 tablespoons pure maple syrup

¼ teaspoon maple extract

1½ cups powdered sugar

Fleur de sel, to taste (optional)

The use of real maple syrup in the frosting of these Maple-Glazed Mini Donuts increases the wonderful depth of flavor. With a delicate vanilla donut as its base, this smooth maple frosting finally gets to be the star!

1. If using an electric donut maker, preheat according to manufacturer's instructions. If using donut pans, preheat oven to 350°F and grease donut pans.

2. In a small bowl, sift together flour, baking powder, and salt. Set aside.

3. In a medium bowl, whisk together egg and sugar. Then, add milk, oil, and vanilla extract, mixing until thoroughly combined. Gently stir in the flour mixture, stirring until there are no lumps.

4. **If using mini-donut pans:** Carefully fill each donut indentation ¾ full. Bake for 7–9 minutes or until a toothpick inserted into a donut comes out clean. Transfer donuts to a cooling rack and cool completely. **If using an electric mini-donut maker:** Carefully fill each donut indentation ¾ full. Bake according to manufacturer's instructions or until a toothpick inserted into a donut comes out clean. Remove donuts from appliance, transfer to a cooling rack, and let cool completely.

5. Place wax paper under a wire rack to collect any drippings for an easy cleanup. Then, in a small bowl, whisk together milk, pure maple syrup, and maple extract. Add powdered sugar, whisking until smooth.

6. Dip the top of each donut into the frosting, then transfer to a wire rack. Lightly sprinkle the tops with fleur de sel if desired and let set for 5 minutes. Serve immediately, or store in an airtight container for up to 3 days.

FLEUR DE SEL

Fleur de sel has been taking the baking world by storm. It may be just salt to some, but others know that fleur de sel is worth the price, with its flaky texture and fancy French heritage. Sprinkling a little fleur de sel on top of the maple frosting will really make these Maple-Glazed Mini Donuts shine!

Powdered Sugar Mini Donut

 YIELDS 30 MINI DONUTS

FOR DONUTS

1⅓ cups all-purpose flour, sifted

2 teaspoons baking powder

¼ teaspoon salt

1 large egg

½ cup granulated sugar

¾ cup whole milk

3 tablespoons vegetable oil

2 teaspoons vanilla extract

FOR TOPPING

½ cup powdered sugar

These tender vanilla-scented donuts are perfect when coated with the traditionally sweet powdered sugar topping. The sound of tossing these donuts in a paper bag is irresistible and will have your family members begging for the first bite!

1. If using an electric donut maker, preheat according to manufacturer's instructions. If using donut pans, preheat oven to 350°F and grease donut pans.
2. In a small bowl, sift together flour, baking powder, and salt. Set aside.
3. In a medium bowl, whisk together egg and sugar. Then, add milk, oil, and vanilla extract, mixing until thoroughly combined. Gently stir in the flour mixture, stirring until there are no lumps.
4. **If using mini-donut pans:** Carefully fill each donut indentation ¾ full. Bake for 7–9 minutes or until a toothpick inserted into a donut comes out clean. Transfer donuts to a cooling rack and cool for 5 minutes. **If using an electric mini-donut maker:** Carefully fill each donut indentation ¾ full. Bake according to manufacturer's instructions or until a toothpick inserted into a donut comes out clean. Remove donuts from appliance, transfer to a cooling rack, and cool for 5 minutes.
5. Once donuts are cooled, place powdered sugar in a brown paper bag or a plastic Ziploc bag. Working with 2 or 3 donuts at a time, shake to coat in powdered sugar. Serve immediately, or store in an airtight container for up to 3 days.

Powdered Sugar Mini Donuts

Chocolate Cake Mini Donut

 YIELDS 28 MINI DONUTS

FOR DONUTS

1⅓ cups all-purpose flour, sifted

½ cup cocoa powder

2 teaspoons baking powder

¼ teaspoon salt

1 large egg

¾ cup granulated sugar

3 tablespoons vegetable oil

¼ cup sour cream

1 teaspoon vanilla extract

½ cup whole milk

FOR ICING

1 tablespoon whole milk

1 teaspoon vanilla extract

1½ cups powdered sugar

Like a fine wine, these mini donuts only get better with age. Surprisingly, these donuts are tasty the first day, but delicious the second day. If you are looking for a make-ahead donut, this is the one for you!

1. If using an electric donut maker, preheat according to manufacturer's instructions. If using donut pans, preheat oven to 350°F and grease donut pans.
2. In a small bowl, sift together flour, cocoa powder, baking powder, and salt. Set aside.
3. In a medium bowl, whisk together egg and sugar. Then, add oil, sour cream, and vanilla extract, mixing until thoroughly combined. Gently stir in the flour mixture, alternating with the milk, stirring until there are no lumps.
4. **If using mini-donut pans:** Carefully fill each donut indentation ¾ full. Bake for 7–9 minutes or until a toothpick inserted into a donut comes out clean. Transfer donuts to a cooling rack and cool completely. **If using an electric mini-donut maker:** Carefully fill each donut indentation ¾ full. Bake according to manufacturer's instructions or until a toothpick inserted into a donut comes out clean. Remove donuts from appliance, transfer to a cooling rack, and let cool 5 minutes.
5. Place wax paper under a wire rack to collect any drippings for an easy cleanup. Then, in a small bowl, whisk together milk and vanilla extract. Add powdered sugar and whisk until smooth.
6. Dip the top of each donut into the icing, transfer to a wire rack, and let set for 5 minutes. Serve immediately, or store in an airtight container for up to 3 days.

GOT YOUR BASES COVERED

With their rich, chocolate flavor and dense texture, these donuts act as the perfect base for just about any topping. For example, imagine these little darlings covered in maple frosting or dipped in smooth salted caramel. So let your imagination run wild, and see what combinations you can come up with!

Chocolate-Glazed Mini Donut

FOR DONUTS

1⅓ cups all-purpose flour, sifted

2 teaspoons baking powder

¼ teaspoon salt

1 large egg

½ cup granulated sugar

¾ cup whole milk

3 tablespoons vegetable oil

2 teaspoons vanilla extract

FOR ICING

4 tablespoons butter

2 tablespoons whole milk

1 tablespoon light corn syrup

2 ounces bittersweet chocolate, roughly chopped

1 cup powdered sugar, sifted

The Chocolate-Glazed Mini Donut is a sign that everything is right in this world. With its perfect mix of a vanilla donut and rich chocolate icing, this donut showcases the perfection of light and dark. It's not too rich, not too boring, but just right!

1. If using an electric donut maker, preheat according to manufacturer's instructions. If using donut pans, preheat oven to 350°F and grease donut pans.
2. In a small bowl, sift together flour, baking powder, and salt. Set aside.
3. In a medium bowl, whisk together egg and sugar. Then add milk, oil, and vanilla extract, mixing until thoroughly combined. Gently stir in the flour mixture, stirring until there are no lumps.
4. **If using mini-donut pans:** Carefully fill each donut indentation ¾ full. Bake for 7–9 minutes or until a toothpick inserted into a donut comes out clean. Transfer donuts to a cooling rack and cool completely. **If using an electric mini-donut maker:** Carefully fill each donut indentation ¾ full. Bake according to manufacturer's instructions or until a toothpick inserted into a donut comes out clean. Remove donuts from appliance, transfer to a cooling rack, and let cool completely.
5. Place wax paper under a wire rack to collect any drippings for an easy cleanup. Then, in a small saucepan over medium heat, melt butter. Add milk, corn syrup, and chopped chocolate, stirring slowly to allow chocolate to melt completely.
6. Once melted, remove from heat and whisk in powdered sugar. Immediately dip the top of each donut into the icing and transfer to a wire rack.
7. Let icing set for 10 minutes and then serve. Donuts can be stored in an airtight container for up to 2 days but are best when eaten fresh.

CHOCOLATE CHIPS!

To add a fun spin on this classic, add ⅓ cup of mini chocolate chips to the batter of these Chocolate-Glazed Mini Donuts. They won't be visible from the outside, but once you bite into the donut, you will find an extra chocolate-y surprise!

Vanilla-Sprinkle Mini Donut

 YIELDS 30 MINI DONUTS

FOR DONUTS

1⅓ cups all-purpose flour, sifted

2 teaspoons baking powder

¼ teaspoon salt

1 large egg

½ cup granulated sugar

¾ cup whole milk

3 tablespoons vegetable oil

2 teaspoons vanilla extract

FOR ICING

1 tablespoon whole milk

1 teaspoon vanilla extract

1½ cups powdered sugar

FOR TOPPING

Sprinkles

Between the colorful sprinkles and the vanilla-scented donut, these classic Vanilla-Sprinkle Mini Donuts are a favorite with kids and adults alike. Maximize the fun by adding theme-colored sprinkles for the holidays!

1. If using an electric donut maker, preheat according to manufacturer's instructions. If using donut pans, preheat oven to 350°F and grease donut pans.
2. In a small bowl, sift together flour, baking powder, and salt. Set aside.
3. In a medium bowl, whisk together egg and sugar. Then, add milk, oil, and vanilla extract, mixing until thoroughly combined. Gently stir in the flour mixture, stirring until there are no lumps.
4. **If using mini-donut pans:** Carefully fill each donut indentation ¾ full. Bake for 7–9 minutes or until a toothpick inserted into a donut comes out clean. Transfer donuts to a cooling rack and cool completely. **If using an electric mini-donut maker:** Carefully fill each donut indentation ¾ full. Bake according to manufacturer's instructions or until a toothpick inserted into a donut comes out clean. Remove donuts from appliance, transfer to a cooling rack, and let cool completely.
5. Place wax paper under a wire rack to collect any drippings for an easy cleanup. Then, in a small bowl, whisk together milk and vanilla extract. Add powdered sugar and whisk until smooth.
6. Dip the top of each donut into the icing and transfer to a wire rack. Adorn the top of each donut with sprinkles and let set for 5 minutes. Serve immediately; donuts can be stored in an airtight container for up to 3 days but are best served fresh.

JIMMIES

The traditional sprinkle used on top of donuts is called a jimmie. It is a long, rod-shaped sprinkle that comes in multicolored or chocolate. It is usually found in the ice cream–toppings aisle at the grocery store but can also be found in the cake-decorating aisle.

Vanilla-Sprinkle Mini Donuts

Blueberry Cake Mini Donut

FOR DONUTS

1¾ cups all-purpose flour, sifted

2 teaspoons baking powder

¼ teaspoon salt

1 large egg

¾ cup granulated sugar

3 tablespoons vegetable oil

¼ cup sour cream

1 teaspoon vanilla extract

½ cup whole milk

½ cup blueberries, chopped

FOR ICING

1 tablespoon whole milk

1 teaspoon vanilla extract

1½ cups powdered sugar

The classic blueberry donut can always be found on a donut shop's shelves. Although it may be a "common" donut, its dense cake texture and beautiful bursts of blueberries make it impossible to overlook!

1. If using an electric donut maker, preheat according to manufacturer's instructions. If using donut pans, preheat oven to 350°F and grease donut pans.
2. In a small bowl, sift together flour, baking powder, and salt. Set aside.
3. In a medium bowl, whisk together egg and sugar. Then add oil, sour cream, and vanilla extract, mixing until thoroughly combined. Gently stir in the flour mixture, alternating with the milk, stirring until there are no lumps. Carefully fold in the chopped blueberries. Transfer batter to a piping bag, or to a Ziploc baggie with a hole cut in the tip.
4. **If using mini-donut pans:** Carefully fill each donut indentation ¾ full. Bake for 7–9 minutes or until a toothpick inserted into a donut comes out clean. Transfer donuts to a cooling rack and cool completely. **If using an electric mini-donut maker:** Carefully fill each donut indentation ¾ full. Bake according to manufacturer's instructions or until a toothpick inserted into a donut comes out clean. Remove donuts from appliance, transfer to a cooling rack, and let cool 5 minutes.
5. Place wax paper under a wire rack to collect any drippings for an easy cleanup. Then, in a small bowl, whisk together milk and vanilla extract. Add powdered sugar and whisk until smooth.
6. Dip the top of each donut into the icing, transfer to a wire rack, and let set for 5 minutes. Serve immediately, or store in an airtight container for up to 2 days.

Strawberry-Frosted Mini Donut

 YIELDS 30 MINI DONUTS

FOR DONUTS

1⅓ cups all-purpose flour, sifted

2 teaspoons baking powder

¼ teaspoon salt

1 large egg

½ cup granulated sugar

¾ cup whole milk

3 tablespoons vegetable oil

2 teaspoons vanilla extract

FOR FROSTING

1 tablespoon whole milk

2 teaspoons strawberry extract

3–4 drops red food coloring

1½ cups powdered sugar

Between the bright pink color and the burst of strawberry flavor, strawberry-frosted donuts are one of the most requested donuts at donut shops across the country. They are immediately recognizable in a donut lineup and are always one of the first to go. Thankfully, with this recipe, you can make these classic donuts at home and avoid the rush!

1. If using an electric donut maker, preheat according to manufacturer's instructions. If using donut pans, preheat oven to 350°F and grease donut pans.

2. In a small bowl, sift together flour, baking powder, and salt. Set aside.

3. In a medium bowl, whisk together egg and sugar. Then add milk, oil, and vanilla extract, mixing until thoroughly combined. Gently stir in the flour mixture, stirring until there are no lumps.

4. **If using mini-donut pans:** Carefully fill each donut indentation ¾ full. Bake for 7–9 minutes or until a toothpick inserted into a donut comes out clean. Transfer donuts to a cooling rack and cool completely. **If using an electric mini-donut maker:** Carefully fill each donut indentation ¾ full. Bake according to manufacturer's instructions or until a toothpick inserted into a donut comes out clean. Remove donuts from appliance, transfer to a cooling rack, and let cool completely.

5. Place wax paper under a wire rack to collect any drippings for an easy cleanup. Then, in a small bowl, whisk together milk, strawberry extract, and red food coloring. Add powdered sugar, whisking until smooth.

6. Dip the top of each donut into the frosting, transfer to a wire rack, and let set for 5 minutes. Serve immediately, or store in an airtight container for up to 3 days.

Chapter 2

CHOCOLATE^2

Chocolate × Chocolate = Chocolate^2—or at least it does in this mini-donut equation. Each of these mini donuts have enough chocolate to satisfy any chocolate lover's sweet tooth. The recipes in this chapter are bursting with a heavy dose of chocolate combined with a fun or outrageous supporting flavor, like chipotle pepper, coconut, or even bacon. But it doesn't matter which of the combinations you choose—these mini donuts will be the shining star on any table!

Dark Chocolate–Ganache Mini Donut

 YIELDS 30 MINI DONUTS

FOR DONUTS

1 cup all-purpose flour, sifted

⅓ cup cocoa powder, sifted

2 teaspoons baking powder

¼ teaspoon salt

1 large egg

½ cup granulated sugar

¾ cup whole milk

2 tablespoons vegetable oil

2 tablespoons sour cream

½ teaspoon vanilla extract

FOR GANACHE

3 ounces dark chocolate (at least 60 percent cocoa), chopped

⅓ cup heavy whipping cream

2 tablespoons granulated sugar

1 tablespoon unsalted butter

There are many flavors of chocolate, ranging from white to milk to semisweet chocolate, but none are as rich—or as decadent—as dark chocolate. The dark chocolate ganache that glazes these mini donuts is so rich that it can be served to only the truest of chocolate fans!

1. If using an electric donut maker, preheat according to manufacturer's instructions. If using donut pans, preheat oven to 350°F and grease donut pans.
2. In a small bowl, sift together flour, cocoa powder, baking powder, and salt. Set aside.
3. In a medium bowl, whisk together egg and sugar. Then add milk, oil, sour cream, and vanilla extract, mixing until thoroughly combined. Gently stir in the flour mixture, stirring until there are no lumps.
4. **If using mini-donut pans:** Carefully fill each donut indentation ¾ full. Bake for 7–9 minutes or until a toothpick inserted into a donut comes out clean. Transfer donuts to a cooling rack and let cool completely. **If using an electric mini-donut maker:** Carefully fill each donut indentation ¾ full. Bake according to manufacturer's instructions or until a toothpick inserted into a donut comes out clean. Remove donuts from appliance, transfer to a cooling rack, and let cool completely.
5. Place chocolate in a medium-sized heatproof bowl and set aside. Heat the cream, sugar, and butter in a small saucepan over medium heat. Bring to a boil and immediately pour the boiling cream over the chocolate. Allow to stand, without stirring, for a few minutes. Then, stir gently (you do not want to incorporate air into the ganache) with a spoon or whisk until smooth.
6. Allow ganache to cool on the counter for about 10 minutes, stirring as needed, until it cools and slightly thickens. Place wax paper under a wire rack to collect any drippings for an easy cleanup. Dip the top of each donut into the ganache and transfer to a wire rack.
7. Let donuts set for 5 minutes and then serve. Donuts can be stored in an airtight container for up to 3 days but are best when eaten fresh.

Dark Chocolate-Ganache Mini Donuts

Chocolate-Buttermilk Mini Donut

 YIELDS 30 MINI DONUTS

FOR DONUTS

1 cup all-purpose flour, sifted

⅓ cup cocoa powder, sifted

2 teaspoons baking powder

½ teaspoon ground cinnamon

¼ teaspoon nutmeg

¼ teaspoon salt

1 large egg

½ cup granulated sugar

½ cup sour cream

¼ cup vegetable oil

1 teaspoon vanilla extract

¾ cup buttermilk

FOR ICING

4 tablespoons butter

2 tablespoons whole milk

1 tablespoon light corn syrup

2 ounces bittersweet chocolate, roughly chopped

1 cup powdered sugar, sifted

A traditional buttermilk donut is slightly scented with nutmeg and cinnamon, but adding chocolate to these little pieces of heaven really makes them stand out! If you are feeling frisky, try using the maple icing (see the Maple-Glazed Mini Donut recipe in Chapter 1) for a funky twist.

1. If using an electric donut maker, preheat according to manufacturer's instructions. If using donut pans, preheat oven to 350°F and grease donut pans.
2. In a small bowl, sift together flour, cocoa powder, baking powder, cinnamon, nutmeg, and salt. Set aside.
3. In a medium bowl, whisk together egg and sugar. Then add sour cream, oil, and vanilla extract, mixing until thoroughly combined. Gently stir in the flour mixture, alternating with the buttermilk, stirring until there are no large lumps.
4. **If using mini-donut pans:** Carefully fill each donut indentation ¾ full. Bake for 7–9 minutes or until a toothpick inserted into a donut comes out clean. Transfer donuts to a cooling rack and let cool completely. **If using an electric mini-donut maker:** Carefully fill each donut indentation ¾ full. Bake according to manufacturer's instructions or until a toothpick inserted into a donut comes out clean. Remove donuts from appliance, transfer to a cooling rack, and let cool completely.
5. Place wax paper under a wire rack to collect any drippings for an easy cleanup. Then, in a small saucepan over medium heat, melt butter. Add milk, corn syrup, and chopped chocolate, stirring slowly to allow chocolate to melt completely.
6. Once melted, remove from heat and whisk in powdered sugar. Immediately dip the top of each donut into the icing and then transfer to a wire rack.
7. Let icing set for 10 minutes and then serve. Donuts can be stored in an airtight container for up to 2 days but are best when eaten fresh.

Chocolate-Glazed Fried Mini Donut

 YIELDS 26 MINI DONUTS AND
MINI DONUT HOLES

FOR DONUTS

2 tablespoons water, warmed

1.25-ounce envelope fast-rise yeast

¾ cup whole milk, warmed

¼ cup granulated sugar

½ teaspoon salt

1 large egg

3 tablespoons shortening or lard

2½ cups all-purpose flour

Vegetable oil or peanut oil, for frying

FOR FROSTING

4 tablespoons butter

2 tablespoons whole milk

1 tablespoon light corn syrup

2 ounces bittersweet chocolate, roughly chopped

1 cup powdered sugar, sifted

These Chocolate-Glazed Fried Mini Donuts are the answer to any problem. Bad day? They are here to comfort you. Hungry? You know they can fix that. Lost your keys again? Well, maybe they can't help with that, but they are the sugary answer to just about anything else!

1. In the bowl of your stand mixer, with the paddle attachment (or in a large bowl if you are going to knead the dough by hand), whisk together warm water and yeast and let stand for 5 minutes.
2. Add milk, sugar, salt, egg, shortening, and 1 cup of flour. Mix on medium-low for 2 minutes, then switch to the dough hook. Slowly add the remaining 1½ cups of flour, ½ cup at a time. Once you have added all the flour, knead on medium for 2–3 minutes, until dough no longer sticks to the bowl. Turn up the speed to medium-high, and continue to knead dough for 3–4 minutes, until dough is smooth.
3. Transfer dough to a greased bowl, and cover with a slightly damp tea towel. Place bowl in a warm area (or in an oven preheated to 200°F and then turned off) for about one hour. Dough is ready when it has doubled in size.
4. Transfer raised dough to a lightly floured surface, and carefully roll out until it is ½" thick. Cut out donuts with a floured 2" biscuit cutter, and then cut out the center of each donut with a floured 1" biscuit cutter.
5. Place donuts and donut holes on a lightly floured cookie sheet, and cover again with a slightly damp tea towel. Place in a warm area (or in an oven preheated to 200°F and then turned off) for about 1 hour. Dough is ready when it has doubled in size.
6. Heat oil in a large, deep skillet or a deep fryer set to 350°F.
7. Once oil is hot, working with 4 to 6 donuts at a time, carefully drop donuts into oil. Fry for 1–2 minutes or until golden brown; flip each donut and fry the other side.
8. Remove and drain on a plate lined with newspaper or paper towels. Continue this process until each donut has been fried.
9. Place wax paper under a wire rack to collect any drippings for an easy cleanup. Then, in a small saucepan over medium heat, melt butter. Add milk, corn syrup, and chopped chocolate, stirring slowly to allow chocolate to melt completely.
10. Once melted, remove from heat and whisk in powdered sugar. Immediately dip the top of each donut into the icing and transfer to a wire rack.
11. Let frosting set for 10 minutes and then serve. Donuts can be stored in an airtight container for up to 2 days but are best when eaten fresh.

Chocolate-Toasted Coconut Mini Donut

Chocolate-Toasted Coconut Mini Donut

YIELDS 30 MINI DONUTS

This little mini donut sure does pack one heck of a coconut punch. Between coconut extract, coconut milk, and toasted coconut on top, it's like a mini coconut explosion! And when you combine that coconut explosion with, of course, chocolate, you're in for a mini donut that will knock your socks off!

FOR DONUTS

1 cup all-purpose flour, sifted

⅓ cup cocoa powder, sifted

2 teaspoons baking powder

¼ teaspoon salt

1 large egg

½ cup granulated sugar

½ cup whole milk

¼ cup coconut milk

2 tablespoons vegetable oil

2 tablespoons sour cream

½ teaspoon coconut extract

FOR ICING

4 tablespoons butter

2 tablespoons coconut milk

1 tablespoon light corn syrup

2 ounces bittersweet chocolate, roughly chopped

FOR TOPPING

1 cup powdered sugar, sifted

1 cup shredded coconut, toasted (for instructions see sidebar, below)

TOASTED COCONUT

To make toasted coconut, preheat oven to 350°F. Spread sweetened shredded coconut on a foil-lined baking sheet and bake for 5 minutes, stirring often, until light golden brown. Let cool, and then use as homemade sprinkles on top of all of your favorite mini donuts!

1. If using an electric donut maker, preheat according to manufacturer's instructions. If using donut pans, preheat oven to 350°F and grease donut pans.
2. In a small bowl, sift together flour, cocoa powder, baking powder, and salt. Set aside.
3. In a medium bowl, whisk together egg and sugar. Then add milk, coconut milk, oil, sour cream, and coconut extract, mixing until thoroughly combined. Gently stir in the flour mixture, stirring until there are no lumps.
4. **If using mini-donut pans:** Carefully fill each donut indentation ¾ full. Bake for 7–9 minutes or until a toothpick inserted into a donut comes out clean. Transfer donuts to a cooling rack and let cool completely. **If using an electric mini-donut maker:** Carefully fill each donut indentation ¾ full. Bake according to manufacturer's instructions or until a toothpick inserted into a donut comes out clean. Remove donuts from appliance, transfer to a cooling rack, and let cool completely.
5. Place wax paper under a wire rack to collect any drippings for an easy cleanup. Then, in a small saucepan over medium heat, melt butter. Add coconut milk, corn syrup, and chopped chocolate, stirring slowly to allow chocolate to melt completely.
6. Once melted, remove from heat and whisk in powdered sugar. Immediately dip the top of each donut into the icing, then dip into the toasted coconut and place on a wire rack to cool.
7. Let icing set for 10 minutes and then serve. Donuts can be stored in an airtight container for up to 2 days but are best when eaten fresh.

Devil's Food Mini Donut

 YIELDS 30 MINI DONUTS

FOR DONUTS

1 cup all-purpose flour, sifted

⅓ cup Dutch-process cocoa powder, sifted

2 teaspoons baking powder

1 teaspoon instant espresso granules

¼ teaspoon salt

1 large egg

¼ cup granulated sugar

¼ cup packed brown sugar

¾ cup whole milk

2 tablespoons vegetable oil

2 tablespoons sour cream

½ teaspoon vanilla extract

FOR GANACHE

3 ounces dark chocolate (at least 60 percent cocoa), chopped

⅓ cup heavy whipping cream

2 tablespoons granulated sugar

1 tablespoon unsalted butter

Devil's food cake is one of the darkest, richest chocolate cakes ever made. These Devil's Food Mini Donuts are made with Dutch-process cocoa powder, instant espresso granules, and brown sugar to ensure they stay dark and devilish!

1. If using an electric donut maker, preheat according to manufacturer's instructions. If using donut pans, preheat oven to 350°F and grease donut pans.
2. In a small bowl, sift together flour, cocoa powder, baking powder, instant espresso granules, and salt. Set aside.
3. In a medium bowl, whisk together egg, granulated sugar, and brown sugar. Then add milk, oil, sour cream, and vanilla extract, mixing until thoroughly combined. Gently stir in the flour mixture, stirring until there are no lumps.
4. **If using mini-donut pans:** Carefully fill each donut indentation ¾ full. Bake for 7–9 minutes or until a toothpick inserted into a donut comes out clean. Transfer donuts to a cooling rack and let cool completely. **If using an electric mini-donut maker:** Carefully fill each donut indentation ¾ full. Bake according to manufacturer's instructions or until a toothpick inserted into a donut comes out clean. Remove donuts from appliance, transfer to a cooling rack, and let cool completely.
5. Place chocolate in a medium-sized heatproof bowl and set aside. Heat the cream, sugar, and butter in a small saucepan over medium heat. Bring to a boil and immediately pour the boiling cream over the chocolate. Allow to stand, without stirring, for a few minutes. Then, stir gently (you do not want to incorporate air into the ganache) with a spoon or whisk until smooth.
6. Allow ganache to cool on the counter for about 10 minutes, stirring as needed, until it cools and slightly thickens. Place wax paper under a wire rack to collect any drippings for an easy cleanup. Dip the top of each donut into the ganache and transfer to a wire rack.
7. Let donuts set for 5 minutes and then serve. Donuts can be stored in an airtight container for up to 3 days but are best when eaten fresh.

White Chocolate–Red Velvet Mini Donut

 YIELDS 18 MINI DONUTS

FOR DONUTS

1 cup all-purpose flour

1 tablespoon cocoa powder

2 teaspoons baking powder

¼ teaspoon salt

½ cup granulated sugar

1 large egg

½ cup buttermilk

2 tablespoons vegetable oil

1 teaspoon vanilla extract

½ teaspoon white distilled vinegar

½ teaspoon red food coloring

FOR FROSTING

2 ounces cream cheese, softened

1 cup powdered sugar

1 tablespoon whole milk

FOR TOPPING

2 ounces white chocolate, shaved

Between the chocolate in the donut batter and the white chocolate shavings on top, this White Chocolate–Red Velvet Mini Donut truly is the epitome of Chocolate². In this recipe, tangy red velvet is combined with creamy cream cheese in this fun spin on the classic red cake.

1. If using an electric donut maker, preheat according to manufacturer's instructions. If using donut pans, preheat oven to 350°F and grease donut pans.
2. In a small bowl, whisk together flour, cocoa powder, baking powder, and salt. Set aside.
3. In a medium bowl, whisk together the sugar and egg. Then add buttermilk, oil, vanilla extract, and vinegar, mixing until thoroughly combined. Gently stir in the flour mixture, stirring until there are no lumps. Slowly add ½ teaspoon red food coloring, adding a few more drops if needed.
4. **If using mini-donut pans:** Carefully fill each donut indentation ¾ full. Bake for 7–9 minutes or until donuts are slightly browned and spring back when touched. Remove from oven, transfer to a cooling rack, and let cool completely. **If using an electric mini-donut maker:** Carefully fill each donut indentation ¾ full. Bake according to manufacturer's instructions or until the donuts are slightly browned and spring back when touched. Transfer donuts to a cooling rack and let cool completely.
5. Place wax paper under a wire rack to collect any drippings for an easy cleanup. Then, in a stand mixer, blend together cream cheese and powdered sugar. Slowly add milk, whisking constantly, until you get a smooth frosting.
6. Dip the top of each donut into the frosting and transfer to a wire rack. Immediately sprinkle the top of each donut with white-chocolate shavings. Let frosting set for 5 minutes and then serve. Donuts can be stored in an airtight container in the refrigerator for up to 2 days but are best when eaten fresh.

Chocolate-Chipotle Mini Donut

FOR DONUTS

1 cup all-purpose flour, sifted

⅓ cup cocoa powder, sifted

2 teaspoons baking powder

½ teaspoon ground chipotle chili pepper

¼ teaspoon salt

1 large egg

½ cup granulated sugar

¾ cup whole milk

2 tablespoons vegetable oil

2 tablespoons sour cream

½ teaspoon vanilla extract

FOR ICING

4 tablespoons butter

2 tablespoons whole milk

1 tablespoon light corn syrup

2 ounces bittersweet chocolate, roughly chopped

1 cup powdered sugar, sifted

¼ teaspoon ground chipotle chili pepper

SOME LIKE IT HOT

Chipotle peppers are actually jalapeño peppers that are ripened until they turn red and then are wood-smoked. Ground chipotle pepper gives a smoky, hot flavor to anything it touches, but in chocolate, the pepper deepens the flavor and provides a wonderful slow burn.

Everyone knows—and loves—the combination of sweet and salty flavors. But where's the love for all things sweet and spicy? Find your passion with these Chocolate-Chipotle Mini Donuts, which have a deep chocolate flavor and a wonderful slow burn at the end to satisfy all of your taste buds.

1. If using an electric donut maker, preheat according to manufacturer's instructions. If using donut pans, preheat oven to 350°F and grease donut pans.

2. In a small bowl, sift together flour, cocoa powder, baking powder, ground chipotle pepper, and salt. Set aside.

3. In a medium bowl, whisk together egg and sugar. Then add milk, oil, sour cream, and vanilla extract, mixing until thoroughly combined. Gently stir in the flour mixture, stirring until there are no lumps.

4. **If using mini-donut pans:** Carefully fill each donut indentation ¾ full. Bake for 7–9 minutes or until a toothpick inserted into a donut comes out clean. Transfer donuts to a cooling rack and let cool completely. **If using an electric mini-donut maker:** Carefully fill each donut indentation ¾ full. Bake according to manufacturer's instructions or until a toothpick inserted into a donut comes out clean. Remove donuts from appliance, transfer to a cooling rack, and let cool completely.

5. Place wax paper under a wire rack to collect any drippings for an easy cleanup. Then, in a small saucepan over medium heat, melt butter. Add milk, corn syrup, and chopped chocolate, stirring slowly to allow chocolate to melt completely.

6. Once melted, remove from heat and whisk in powdered sugar and ground chipotle pepper. Immediately dip the top of each donut into the icing and transfer to a wire rack.

7. Let frosting set for 10 minutes and then serve. Donuts can be stored in an airtight container for up to 2 days but are best when eaten fresh.

Chocolate-Chipotle Mini Donuts

Nutella Mini Donut

 YIELDS 30 MINI DONUTS

FOR DONUTS

1 cup all-purpose flour

2 teaspoons baking powder

¼ teaspoon salt

¼ cup Nutella

½ cup granulated sugar

1 large egg

¾ cup whole milk

2 tablespoons vegetable oil

FOR FROSTING

2 tablespoons Nutella

½ cup powdered sugar

1 tablespoon whole milk

Hazelnuts are one of the greatest complements to chocolate, but they are incredibly hard to find anytime besides the holidays. Thankfully, Nutella— the perfect combination of hazelnut and chocolate in a delicious spread—is available year round. These Nutella Mini Donuts are the perfect way to serve up a scrumptious dose of your favorite chocolate hazelnut spread!

1. If using an electric donut maker, preheat according to manufacturer's instructions. If using donut pans, preheat oven to 350°F and grease donut pans.
2. In a small bowl, whisk together flour, baking powder, and salt. Set aside.
3. In a medium bowl, cream together Nutella and sugar. Carefully add egg, milk, and oil, mixing until thoroughly combined. Then, alternating the flour mixture and milk, combine all ingredients until there are no lumps.
4. **If using mini-donut pans:** Carefully fill each donut indentation ¾ full. Bake for 7–9 minutes or until donuts spring back when touched. Remove from oven, transfer to a cooling rack, and let cool completely. **If using an electric mini-donut maker:** Carefully fill each donut indentation ¾ full. Bake according to manufacturer's instructions or until the donuts spring back when touched. Transfer donuts to a cooling rack and let cool completely.
5. Place wax paper under a wire rack to collect any drippings for an easy cleanup. Then, in a small bowl, whisk together Nutella and powdered sugar. Slowly add milk, whisking constantly, until you get a smooth frosting.
6. Dip the top of each donut into the frosting and transfer to a wire rack. Let frosting set for 5 minutes and then serve. Donuts can be refrigerated in an airtight container for up to 3 days but are best when eaten fresh.

BISCOFF SPREAD

Biscoff has a delicious spread, made from Biscoff cookies (sometimes called "The Airline Cookie"), that is comparable to the texture of Nutella. It makes a perfect substitute in this recipe; just swap Biscoff Spread for Nutella, and enjoy a Biscoff cookie–flavored mini donut!

Chocolate-Bacon-Maple Mini Donut

 YIELDS 30 MINI DONUTS

FOR DONUTS

1 cup all-purpose flour, sifted

¼ cup cocoa powder, sifted

2 teaspoons baking powder

1 teaspoon instant espresso granules

¼ teaspoon salt

1 large egg

½ cup granulated sugar

¾ cup whole milk

3 tablespoons vegetable oil

1 teaspoon vanilla extract

FOR FROSTING

½ teaspoon whole milk

2 tablespoons pure maple syrup

¼ teaspoon maple extract

1½ cups powdered sugar

8 strips center-cut bacon, cooked and crumbled

THE REAL STUFF

There is a big difference between pure maple syrup and pancake syrup. While you may want to reach for the cheap alternative, take a risk and splurge for the good stuff! Pancake syrups are made with corn syrup and artificial flavorings, which make them thick and extremely sticky. Pure maple syrup has a strong maple flavor and is a thin, easy-to-pour liquid.

Although not a traditional combination, chocolate and bacon desserts have been taking over the culinary world. And why not? The salty, smoky bacon and the rich chocolate donut are a match made in heaven. But when you add in the sweet maple frosting, you have a donut that is seriously out of this world!

1. If using an electric donut maker, preheat according to manufacturer's instructions. If using donut pans, preheat oven to 350°F and grease donut pans.

2. In a small bowl, sift together flour, cocoa powder, baking powder, instant espresso granules, and salt. Set aside.

3. In a medium bowl, whisk together egg and sugar. Then add milk, oil, and vanilla extract, mixing until thoroughly combined. Gently stir in the flour mixture, stirring until there are no lumps.

4. **If using mini-donut pans:** Carefully fill each donut indentation ¾ full. Bake for 7–9 minutes or until a toothpick inserted into a donut comes out clean. Transfer donuts to a cooling rack and let cool completely. **If using an electric mini-donut maker:** Carefully fill each donut indentation ¾ full. Bake according to manufacturer's instructions or until a toothpick inserted into a donut comes out clean. Remove donuts from appliance, transfer to a cooling rack, and let cool completely.

5. Place wax paper under a wire rack to collect any drippings for an easy cleanup. Then, in a small bowl, whisk together milk, pure maple syrup, and maple extract. Add powdered sugar, whisking until smooth.

6. Dip the top of each donut into the frosting, transfer to a wire rack, and sprinkle with crumbled bacon. Let set for 5 minutes and then serve. Donuts are best served fresh but can be stored in an airtight container in the refrigerator for up to 3 days.

German Chocolate Mini Donuts

German Chocolate Mini Donut

 YIELDS 30 MINI DONUTS

FOR DONUTS

1 cup all-purpose flour, sifted

¼ cup cocoa powder, sifted

2 teaspoons baking powder

1 teaspoon instant espresso granules

¼ teaspoon salt

1 large egg

½ cup granulated sugar

¼ cup buttermilk

½ cup whole milk

3 tablespoons vegetable oil

1 teaspoon vanilla extract

FOR FROSTING

⅓ cup granulated sugar

5 ounces evaporated milk

3 tablespoons butter

1 large egg yolk

1 cup shredded coconut

½ cup chopped pecans

½ teaspoon vanilla extract

While the name suggests otherwise, German Chocolate cake was dreamed up by an American many, many years ago. But while the first German Chocolate cake was made when petticoats were still in style, the rich flavors still have a place in our hearts today. These German Chocolate Mini Donuts are the perfect way to honor the classic cake!

1. If using an electric donut maker, preheat according to manufacturer's instructions. If using donut pans, preheat oven to 350°F and grease donut pans.
2. In a small bowl, sift together flour, cocoa powder, baking powder, instant espresso granules, and salt. Set aside.
3. In a medium bowl, whisk together egg and sugar. Then add buttermilk, milk, oil, and vanilla extract, mixing until thoroughly combined. Gently stir in the flour mixture, stirring until there are no lumps.
4. **If using mini-donut pans:** Carefully fill each donut indentation ¾ full. Bake for 7–9 minutes or until a toothpick inserted into a donut comes out clean. Transfer donuts to a cooling rack.
If using an electric mini-donut maker: Carefully fill each donut indentation ¾ full. Bake according to manufacturer's instructions or until a toothpick inserted into a donut comes out clean. Remove donuts from appliance and transfer to a cooling rack.
5. In a medium saucepan, combine sugar, evaporated milk, butter, and egg yolk. Cook over medium-low heat, stirring constantly until thickened, about 10 minutes. Remove from heat. Stir in coconut, pecans, and vanilla extract. Cool until thick enough to spread.
6. Frost the top of each donut and serve immediately. Donuts are best served fresh but can be stored in an airtight container for up to 3 days.

Black Forest Mini Donut

 YIELDS 30 MINI DONUTS

To all the cherry-and-chocolate fans out there, these Black Forest Mini Donuts are for you! The Black Forest Cake originated in Germany where it is made with their cherry brandy, kirschwasser. In honor of the traditional Black Forest cake, these mini donuts are made the true German way . . . with a smooth dose of kirschwasser!

FOR DONUTS

1 cup all-purpose flour, sifted

¼ cup cocoa powder, sifted

2 teaspoons baking powder

1 teaspoon instant espresso granules

¼ teaspoon salt

1 large egg

½ cup granulated sugar

⅔ cup whole milk

3 tablespoons vegetable oil

1 tablespoon kirschwasser (cherry brandy)

1 teaspoon vanilla extract

FOR ICING

4 tablespoons butter

2 tablespoons whole milk

1 tablespoon light corn syrup

2 ounces bittersweet chocolate, roughly chopped

1 cup powdered sugar, sifted

¾ cup heavy whipping cream

2 teaspoons kirschwasser (cherry brandy)

½ teaspoon vanilla extract

3 tablespoons powdered sugar

FOR TOPPING

30 maraschino cherries

1. If using an electric donut maker, preheat according to manufacturer's instructions. If using donut pans, preheat oven to 350°F and grease donut pans.
2. In a small bowl, sift together flour, cocoa powder, baking powder, instant espresso granules, and salt. Set aside.
3. In a medium bowl, whisk together egg and sugar. Then add milk, oil, kirschwasser, and vanilla extract, mixing until thoroughly combined. Gently stir in the flour mixture, stirring until there are no lumps.
4. **If using mini-donut pans:** Carefully fill each donut indentation ¾ full. Bake for 7–9 minutes or until a toothpick inserted into a donut comes out clean. Transfer donuts to a cooling rack and let cool completely. **If using an electric mini-donut maker:** Carefully fill each donut indentation ¾ full. Bake according to manufacturer's instructions or until a toothpick inserted into a donut comes out clean. Remove donuts from appliance, transfer to a cooling rack, and let cool completely.
5. Place wax paper under a wire rack to collect any drippings for an easy cleanup. Then, in a small saucepan over medium heat, melt butter. Add milk, corn syrup, and chopped chocolate, stirring slowly to allow chocolate to melt completely.
6. Once melted, remove from heat and whisk in powdered sugar. Immediately dip the top of each donut into the icing and transfer to a wire rack. Let cool for 10 minutes.
7. In a stand mixer, whip cream until peaks are just starting to form. Add in kirschwasser, vanilla extract, and powdered sugar, and continue beating until stiff peaks form. Transfer whipped cream to a piping bag, and pipe onto the tops of the cooled chocolate layer.
8. Top each donut with a maraschino cherry and serve immediately. These donuts do not store well and should be eaten fresh.

Black Forest Mini Donut

Rocky Road Mini Donut

 YIELDS 30 MINI DONUTS

FOR DONUTS

1 cup all-purpose flour, sifted

⅓ cup cocoa powder, sifted

2 teaspoons baking powder

¼ teaspoon salt

1 large egg

½ cup granulated sugar

¾ cup whole milk

2 tablespoons vegetable oil

2 tablespoons sour cream

½ teaspoon vanilla extract

¼ cup walnuts, chopped

FOR ICING

4 tablespoons butter

2 tablespoons whole milk

1 tablespoon light corn syrup

2 ounces bittersweet chocolate, roughly chopped

1 cup powdered sugar, sifted

½ cup mini marshmallows

¼ cup walnuts, chopped

GO NUTTY!

Although the recipe calls for walnuts, break out of the box and top this mini donut with your favorite nuts instead! Pecans, almonds, peanuts, or even pistachios would be great substitutions. Go wild and make it your own!

Rocky road may have started out as a famous ice cream, but it was just made to be a donut. Topping a chocolate donut with a dark chocolate icing is good, but sprinkling chopped walnuts and mini marshmallows on top takes these mini donuts from good to unbelievably awesome!

1. If using an electric donut maker, preheat according to manufacturer's instructions. If using donut pans, preheat oven to 350°F and grease donut pans.
2. In a small bowl, sift together flour, cocoa powder, baking powder, and salt. Set aside.
3. In a medium bowl, whisk together egg and sugar. Then add milk, oil, sour cream, and vanilla extract, mixing until thoroughly combined. Stir in the flour mixture, stirring until there are no lumps. Gently fold in chopped walnuts.
4. **If using mini-donut pans:** Carefully fill each donut indentation ¾ full. Bake for 7–9 minutes or until a toothpick inserted into a donut comes out clean. Transfer donuts to a cooling rack and let cool completely. **If using an electric mini-donut maker:** Carefully fill each donut indentation ¾ full. Bake according to manufacturer's instructions or until a toothpick inserted into a donut comes out clean. Remove donuts from appliance, transfer to a cooling rack, and let cool completely.
5. Place wax paper under a wire rack to collect any drippings for an easy cleanup. Then, in a small saucepan over medium heat, melt butter. Add milk, corn syrup, and chopped chocolate, stirring slowly to allow chocolate to melt completely.
6. Once melted, remove from heat and whisk in powdered sugar. Immediately dip the top of each donut into the icing and transfer to a wire rack.
7. Sprinkle the top of each donut with mini marshmallows and chopped walnuts. Let frosting set for 10 minutes and then serve. Donuts can be stored in an airtight container for up to 2 days but are best when eaten fresh.

Chapter 3

FRUITY

The mini donuts that you are about to discover in this chapter are full of light, fresh flavors that will make your taste buds dance. The recipes were specifically designed to showcase many of your favorite fruits; simply by using strawberries, pineapple, lemons, and more in these sweet mini donuts, you can easily whip up some greatness in your kitchen. And it doesn't matter whether you have gorgeous fresh fruit from your local farmers' market or frozen fruit from two years ago, these mini donuts know how to maximize their fruity impact. In addition, by highlighting the beautiful colors and one-of-a kind flavors from the produce aisle, these mini donuts manage to pack in a few hidden vitamins and minerals. With outrageous flavors like Lemon Meringue Mini Donuts and Coconut-Lime Mini Donuts, you are sure to find a favorite that you can't possibly live without!

Key Lime Pie Mini Donut

 YIELDS 24 MINI DONUTS

FOR DONUTS

½ cup crushed graham crackers

1 tablespoon butter, melted

2 teaspoons sugar

⅔ cup whole milk

2 tablespoons sour cream

1½ cups all-purpose flour, sifted

1½ teaspoons baking powder

¼ teaspoon salt

6 tablespoons butter, room temperature

½ cup granulated sugar

1 large egg

2 tablespoons Key lime juice

Zest of 2 Key limes

FOR ICING

1½ tablespoons Key lime juice

½ teaspoon Key lime zest

1 cup powdered sugar

Contrary to popular belief, there are actually many different types of limes. The two most popular are the Key lime and the regular large lime. A Key lime is the size and shape of a golf ball and is usually light in color, while a traditional lime is a slightly smaller, green version of a lemon. Both versions are easy to find in any supermarket, so it doesn't matter whether you are in Ohio or Florida. With these Key Lime Pie Mini Donuts, you can almost feel the sunshine and smell the palm trees. And you can definitely taste the lime!

1. If using an electric donut maker, preheat according to manufacturer's instructions. If using donut pans, preheat oven to 350°F and grease donut pans.
2. In a small bowl, combine crushed graham crackers, butter, and sugar until crumbly. Set aside.
3. In a small bowl, whisk together milk and sour cream. Set aside. In a separate small bowl, whisk together flour, baking powder, and salt. Set aside.
4. In a large bowl or a stand mixer, cream together butter and sugar until light and fluffy—about 1 minute. Add egg, Key lime juice, and Key lime zest. Beat for 30 seconds, scraping down the bowl as needed.
5. Then, alternating flour mixture and milk mixture, combine all ingredients until just blended. Transfer batter to a piping bag, or to a Ziploc bag with the tip cut off.
6. **If using mini-donut pans:** Carefully fill each donut indentation ¾ full. Top each mini donut with a sprinkle of crushed graham cracker mixture, and gently press into batter. Bake for 7–9 minutes or until a toothpick inserted into a donut comes out clean. Transfer donuts to a cooling rack and cool completely. **If using an electric mini-donut maker:** Carefully fill each donut indentation ¾ full. Top each mini donut with a sprinkle of crushed graham cracker mixture, and gently press into batter. Bake according to manufacturer's instructions or until a toothpick inserted into a donut comes out clean. Remove donuts from appliance, transfer to a cooling rack, and let cool completely.
7. Place wax paper under a wire rack to collect any drippings for an easy cleanup. Then, in a small bowl, whisk together Key lime juice, Key lime zest, and powdered sugar until smooth.
8. Dip the top of each donut into the icing, transfer to a wire rack, and let set for 5 minutes. Serve immediately; donuts can be stored in an airtight container for up to 3 days but are best served fresh.

Strawberry Cream Mini Donut

 YIELDS 24 MINI DONUTS

FOR DONUTS

⅔ cup whole milk

2 tablespoons sour cream

1½ cups all-purpose flour, sifted

1½ teaspoons baking powder

¼ teaspoon salt

6 tablespoons butter, room temperature

½ cup granulated sugar

1 large egg

1 teaspoon strawberry extract

1 cup powdered sugar

FOR ICING

1½ cups powdered sugar

4 large strawberries

1 tablespoon heavy cream

The wonderfully sweet flavor from the strawberries and the rich, smooth texture from the cream make these Strawberry Cream Mini Donuts a match made in heaven. With a scrumptious strawberry-scented donut and a vibrant pink, creamy strawberry frosting, these are sure to win the hearts of any strawberry haters!

1. If using an electric donut maker, preheat according to manufacturer's instructions. If using donut pans, preheat oven to 350°F and grease donut pans.
2. In a small bowl, whisk together milk and sour cream. Set aside. In a separate small bowl, whisk together flour, baking powder, and salt. Set aside.
3. In a large bowl or a stand mixer, cream together butter and sugar until light and fluffy—about 1 minute. Add egg and strawberry extract. Beat for 30 seconds, scraping down the bowl as needed.
4. Then, alternating flour mixture and milk mixture, combine all ingredients until just blended. Transfer batter to a piping bag, or to a Ziploc bag with the tip cut off.
5. **If using mini-donut pans:** Carefully fill each donut indentation ¾ full. Bake for 7–9 minutes or until a toothpick inserted into a donut comes out clean. Transfer donuts to a cooling rack and cool completely. **If using an electric mini-donut maker:** Carefully fill each donut indentation ¾ full. Bake according to manufacturer's instructions or until a toothpick inserted into a donut comes out clean. Remove donuts from appliance, transfer to a cooling rack, and let cool completely.
6. Place wax paper under a wire rack to collect any drippings for an easy cleanup. Then, in a food processor or blender, purée together powdered sugar, strawberries, and heavy cream until a smooth icing forms.
7. Dip the top of each donut into the icing, transfer to a wire rack, and let set for 5 minutes. Serve immediately; donuts can be stored in an airtight container for up to 1 day but are best served fresh.

Lemon-Poppy Seed Mini Donut

 YIELDS 24 MINI DONUTS

FOR DONUTS

⅔ cup whole milk

2 tablespoons sour cream

1½ cups all-purpose flour, sifted

1½ teaspoons baking powder

¼ teaspoon salt

6 tablespoons butter, room temperature

½ cup granulated sugar

1 large egg

Zest of 1 large lemon

1 tablespoon poppy seeds

FOR ICING

2 tablespoons fresh lemon juice

1½ cups powdered sugar

Between their polka-dot style and their burst of lemon flavor, these mini donuts are party ready. Dress up your brunch table with a big pile of these adorable Lemon–Poppy Seed Mini Donuts. Your guests will thank you!

1. If using an electric donut maker, preheat according to manufacturer's instructions. If using donut pans, preheat oven to 350°F and grease donut pans.
2. In a small bowl, whisk together milk and sour cream. Set aside. In a separate small bowl, whisk together flour, baking powder, and salt. Set aside.
3. In a large bowl or a stand mixer, cream together butter and sugar until light and fluffy—about 1 minute. Add egg, lemon zest, and poppy seeds. Beat for 30 seconds, scraping down the bowl as needed.
4. Then, alternating flour mixture and milk mixture, combine all ingredients until just blended. Transfer batter to a piping bag, or to a Ziploc bag with the tip cut off.
5. **If using mini-donut pans:** Carefully fill each donut indentation ¾ full. Bake for 7–9 minutes or until a toothpick inserted into a donut comes out clean. Transfer donuts to a cooling rack and cool completely. **If using an electric mini-donut maker:** Carefully fill each donut indentation ¾ full. Bake according to manufacturer's instructions or until a toothpick inserted into a donut comes out clean. Remove donuts from appliance, transfer to a cooling rack, and let cool completely.
6. Place wax paper under a wire rack to collect any drippings for an easy cleanup. Then, in a small bowl, whisk together lemon juice and powdered sugar until smooth.
7. Dip the top of each donut into the icing, transfer to a wire rack, and let set for 5 minutes. Serve immediately; donuts can be stored in an airtight container for up to 3 days but are best served fresh.

....

DOUBLE DIP

While it's not okay at parties, when you're icing donuts, it is totally acceptable to double dip. If you are a big fan of lemon, circle back around after your first donut dip . . . and dip them again! Just allow a little extra time, about 5 minutes, for the icing to set up after your second dip.

Blueberry-Lemon Mini Donut

 YIELDS 24 MINI DONUTS

FOR DONUTS

⅔ cup whole milk

2 tablespoons sour cream

1½ cups all-purpose flour, sifted

1½ teaspoons baking powder

¼ teaspoon salt

6 tablespoons butter, room temperature

½ cup granulated sugar

1 large egg

2 tablespoons lemon juice

Zest of 1 large lemon

FOR ICING

1½ cups powdered sugar

¼ cup blueberries

Blueberries are known for their sweet bursts of delicious flavor, but when they are combined with the bright citrus flavor of the lemons found here, well, magic happens! These mini donuts go quick, so you might want to consider making more than one batch.

1. If using an electric donut maker, preheat according to manufacturer's instructions. If using donut pans, preheat oven to 350°F and grease donut pans.
2. In a small bowl, whisk together milk and sour cream. Set aside. In a separate small bowl, whisk together flour, baking powder, and salt. Set aside.
3. In a large bowl or a stand mixer, cream together butter and sugar until light and fluffy—about 1 minute. Add egg, lemon juice, and lemon zest. Beat for 30 seconds, scraping down the bowl as needed.
4. Then, alternating flour mixture and milk mixture, combine all ingredients until just blended. Transfer batter to a piping bag, or to a Ziploc bag with the tip cut off.
5. **If using mini-donut pans:** Carefully fill each donut indentation ¾ full. Bake for 7–9 minutes or until a toothpick inserted into a donut comes out clean. Transfer donuts to a cooling rack and cool completely. **If using an electric mini-donut maker:** Carefully fill each donut indentation ¾ full. Bake according to manufacturer's instructions or until a toothpick inserted into a donut comes out clean. Remove donuts from appliance, transfer to a cooling rack, and let cool completely.
6. Place wax paper under a wire rack to collect any drippings for an easy cleanup. Then, in a food processor or blender, purée together powdered sugar and blueberries until a smooth icing forms.
7. Dip the top of each donut into the icing, transfer to a wire rack, and let set for 5 minutes. Serve immediately; donuts can be stored in an airtight container for up to 1 day but are best served fresh.

Chocolate-Tangerine Mini Donuts

Chocolate-Tangerine Mini Donut

 YIELDS 28 MINI DONUTS

FOR DONUTS

1⅓ cups all-purpose flour, sifted

½ cup cocoa powder

2 teaspoons baking powder

¼ teaspoon salt

1 large egg

¾ cup granulated sugar

2 teaspoons tangerine zest

1 tablespoon tangerine juice

3 tablespoons vegetable oil

¼ cup sour cream

1 teaspoon vanilla extract

½ cup whole milk

FOR TOPPING

½ cup granulated sugar

2 tablespoons tangerine zest

FOR ICING

1 tablespoon whole milk

1 teaspoon vanilla extract

1½ cups powdered sugar

GETTIN' ZESTY WITH IT

When grating a fruit for zest, be sure to grate only the colored outside layer of the fruit. Do not grate the white layer, called the pith, that is under the colored skin. The pith is very bitter and will give your mini donuts a bitter aftertaste.

If you are looking for some sparkle and glam, these Chocolate-Tangerine Mini Donuts are your Holy Grail. Not only do the flavors shine, but the glistening tangerine sugar on top makes a real statement, too!

1. If using an electric donut maker, preheat according to manufacturer's instructions. If using donut pans, preheat oven to 350°F and grease donut pans.
2. In a small bowl, sift together flour, cocoa powder, baking powder, and salt. Set aside.
3. In a medium bowl, whisk together egg and sugar. Then add tangerine zest, tangerine juice, oil, sour cream, and vanilla extract, mixing until thoroughly combined. Gently stir in the flour mixture, alternating with the milk, stirring until there are no lumps.
4. **If using mini-donut pans:** Carefully fill each donut indentation ¾ full. Bake for 7–9 minutes or until a toothpick inserted into a donut comes out clean. Transfer donuts to a cooling rack and cool completely. **If using an electric mini-donut maker:** Carefully fill each donut indentation ¾ full. Bake according to manufacturer's instructions or until a toothpick inserted into a donut comes out clean. Remove donuts from appliance, transfer to a cooling rack, and let cool 5 minutes.
5. In a small bowl, combine sugar and tangerine zest with your fingers until zest is evenly distributed; set aside. Place wax paper under a wire rack to collect any drippings for an easy cleanup.
6. Then, in a small bowl, whisk together milk and vanilla extract. Add powdered sugar and whisk until smooth. Dip the top of each donut into the icing and transfer to a wire rack. Immediately sprinkle the tops with the sugar and zest mixture.
7. Let donuts set for 5 minutes and then serve, or store in an airtight container for up to 2 days.

Blackberry Crumble Mini Donut

 YIELDS 28 MINI DONUTS

Whether they're found in the form of a pie, cobbler, or mini donut, black-berries are simply meant to be eaten in some form of a crumble. These Blackberry Crumble Mini Donuts are topped with a beautiful brown sugar–cinnamon crumble that really makes the blackberries shine!

FOR DONUTS

1¾ cups all-purpose flour, sifted

2 teaspoons baking powder

¼ teaspoon salt

1 large egg

¾ cup granulated sugar

3 tablespoons vegetable oil

¼ cup sour cream

1 teaspoon vanilla extract

½ cup whole milk

½ cup blackberries, minced

2 tablespoons butter, melted

¼ cup packed brown sugar

¼ cup flour

¼ teaspoon cinnamon

FOR ICING

2 teaspoons whole milk

½ teaspoon vanilla extract

¾ cup powdered sugar

1. If using an electric donut maker, preheat according to manufacturer's instructions. If using donut pans, preheat oven to 350°F and grease donut pans.
2. In a small bowl, sift together flour, baking powder, and salt. Set aside.
3. In a medium bowl, whisk together egg and sugar. Then add oil, sour cream, and vanilla extract, mixing until thoroughly combined. Gently stir in the flour mixture, alternating with the milk, stirring until there are no lumps. Carefully fold in the minced blackberries. Transfer batter to a piping bag, or to a Ziploc baggie with a hole cut in the tip.
4. In a small bowl, mix together melted butter, brown sugar, flour, and cinnamon. Fluff with a fork until crumbly.
5. **If using mini-donut pans:** Carefully fill each donut indentation ½ full. Generously sprinkle the tops with the crumbly brown-sugar topping. Bake for 7–9 minutes or until a toothpick inserted into a donut comes out clean. Transfer donuts to a cooling rack and cool completely.
   If using an electric mini-donut maker: Carefully fill each donut indentation ½ full. Generously sprinkle the tops with the crumbly brown sugar topping. Bake according to manufacturer's instructions or until a toothpick inserted into a donut comes out clean. Remove donuts from appliance, transfer to a cooling rack, and let cool 5 minutes.
6. Place wax paper under a wire rack to collect any drippings for an easy cleanup. Then, in a small bowl, whisk together milk and vanilla extract. Add powdered sugar and whisk until smooth.
7. Drizzle the top of each donut with the icing, transfer to a wire rack, and let set for 5 minutes. Serve immediately, or store in an airtight container for up to 2 days.

Blackberry Crumble Mini Donuts

Apple Fritter

FOR FRITTERS

1 cup all-purpose flour

1½ teaspoons baking powder

1 teaspoon cinnamon

½ teaspoon salt

¼ teaspoon nutmeg

1 large egg

⅓ cup granulated sugar

½ teaspoon vanilla extract

⅓ cup whole milk

1 heaping cup peeled and chopped apple

Vegetable oil or peanut oil, for frying

FOR ICING

1 tablespoon whole milk

1½ teaspoons vanilla extract

¾ cup powdered sugar

With their crispy outsides and fluffy cinnamon-and-apple-filled insides, these Apple Fritters are one of the best of their kind. Top them with powdered sugar or the classic sticky glaze given here—either is just delicious!

1. Heat oil in a large, deep skillet or a deep fryer to 350°F.
2. In a small bowl, sift together flour, baking powder, cinnamon, salt, and nutmeg. Set aside.
3. In a medium bowl, whisk together egg and granulated sugar. Then add vanilla extract and milk, mixing until thoroughly combined. Gently stir in the flour mixture, stirring until there are no lumps. Gently fold in chopped apple.
4. Once oil is hot, working with 4 to 6 fritters at a time, carefully drop rounded tablespoon of dough into oil. Fry for 1–2 minutes or until golden brown; flip each donut and fry the other side.
5. Remove and drain on a plate lined with newspaper or paper towels. Continue this process until each fritter has been fried.
6. Place wax paper under a wire rack to collect any drippings for an easy cleanup. Then, in a small bowl, whisk together milk and vanilla extract. Add powdered sugar, whisking until smooth.
7. While the fritters are still warm, dip the top of each fritter into the icing, transfer to the wire rack, and let set for 2 minutes. Serve immediately; fritters can be stored in an airtight container for up to 3 days but are best served fresh.

Raspberry-Buttermilk Mini Donut

 YIELDS 28 MINI DONUTS

FOR DONUTS

1⅓ cups all-purpose flour, sifted

2 teaspoons baking powder

½ teaspoon ground cinnamon

¼ teaspoon nutmeg

¼ teaspoon salt

1 large egg

½ cup granulated sugar

½ cup sour cream

¼ cup vegetable oil

1 teaspoon vanilla extract

¾ cup buttermilk

½ cup raspberries, chopped

FOR ICING

1½ cups powdered sugar

¼ cup raspberries

In this recipe, the unique flavors of both raspberries and buttermilk combine to make one exceptional mini donut. This recipe starts with the traditional buttermilk donut and adds a handful of sweet raspberries to the batter to create that wonderful balance of sweet and tangy. Then for good measure, you top these babies off with a healthy dose of raspberry icing! Delicious!

1. If using an electric donut maker, preheat according to manufacturer's instructions. If using donut pans, preheat oven to 350°F and grease donut pans.

2. In a small bowl, sift together flour, baking powder, cinnamon, nutmeg, and salt. Set aside.

3. In a medium bowl, whisk together egg and sugar. Then add sour cream, oil, and vanilla extract, mixing until thoroughly combined. Gently stir in the flour mixture, alternating with the buttermilk, stirring until there are no large lumps. Carefully fold in chopped raspberries.

4. **If using mini-donut pans:** Carefully fill each donut indentation ¾ full. Bake for 7–9 minutes or until a toothpick inserted into a donut comes out clean. Transfer donuts to a cooling rack and let cool completely. **If using an electric mini-donut maker:** Carefully fill each donut indentation ¾ full. Bake according to manufacturer's instructions or until a toothpick inserted into a donut comes out clean. Remove donuts from appliance, transfer to a cooling rack, and let cool completely.

5. Place wax paper under a wire rack to collect any drippings for an easy cleanup. Then, in a food processor or blender, purée together powdered sugar and raspberries until a smooth icing forms.

6. Dip the top of each donut into the icing, transfer to a wire rack, and let set for 5 minutes. Serve immediately; donuts can be stored in an airtight container for up to 1 day but are best served fresh.

Lemon Meringue Mini Donut

FOR DONUTS

⅔ cup whole milk

2 tablespoons sour cream

1½ cups all-purpose flour, sifted

1½ teaspoons baking powder

¼ teaspoon salt

6 tablespoons butter, room temperature

½ cup granulated sugar

1 large egg

2 tablespoons lemon juice

Zest of 1 large lemon

FOR TOPPING

⅓ cup lemon curd

FOR MERINGUE

¾ cup plus 1 tablespoon granulated sugar

⅓ cup water

1 tablespoon light corn syrup

3 large egg whites

> **LEMON CURD**
>
> If you're wandering the aisles of your local grocery store looking for lemon curd, you'll find it sold near the jellies and jams.

For this recipe, a beautiful lemon cake donut is topped with a dollop of lemon curd and finished with a swirl of meringue frosting in a recreation of the classic pie. Who knew such greatness could exist?

1. If using an electric donut maker, preheat according to manufacturer's instructions. If using donut pans, preheat oven to 350°F and grease donut pans.
2. In a small bowl, whisk together milk and sour cream. Set aside. In a separate small bowl, whisk together flour, baking powder, and salt. Set aside.
3. In a large bowl or a stand mixer, cream together butter and sugar until light and fluffy, approximately 1 minute. Add egg, lemon juice, and lemon zest. Beat for 30 seconds, scraping down the bowl as needed.
4. Then, alternating flour mixture and milk mixture, combine all ingredients until just blended. Transfer batter to a piping bag, or to a Ziploc bag with the tip cut off.
5. **If using mini-donut pans:** Carefully fill each donut indentation ¾ full. Bake for 7–9 minutes or until a toothpick inserted into a donut comes out clean. Transfer donuts to a cooling rack and cool completely. **If using an electric mini-donut maker:** Carefully fill each donut indentation ¾ full. Bake according to manufacturer's instructions or until a toothpick inserted into a donut comes out clean. Remove donuts from appliance, transfer to a cooling rack, and let cool completely.
6. Generously apply a thick layer of lemon curd on top of the cooled donuts. Set aside. Then, in a small saucepan over medium heat, melt ¾ cup sugar, water, and corn syrup. Bring to a boil, stirring occasionally, until the syrup reaches 230°F on a candy thermometer.
7. While waiting for the syrup to reach the correct temperature, whisk egg whites on medium-high speed in a stand mixer until soft peaks form. With mixer still running, add remaining 1 tablespoon sugar, whisking to combine.
8. Once sugar reaches 230°F, remove from heat and, with the stand mixer turned on at medium-low speed, slowly pour syrup down the side of the bowl into the egg whites. Raise speed to medium-high, and whisk until mixture is completely cool and stiff peaks form. Transfer to a piping bag, or to a Ziploc bag with the tip cut off, and pipe onto the top of the lemon curd.
9. If you have a kitchen torch, slightly brown the tops of the meringue. Serve immediately; these mini donuts do not store well.

Cranberry-Orange Mini Donut

 YIELDS 24 MINI DONUTS

FOR DONUTS

⅔ cup whole milk

2 tablespoons sour cream

1½ cups all-purpose flour, sifted

1½ teaspoons baking powder

¼ teaspoon salt

6 tablespoons butter, room temperature

½ cup granulated sugar

1 large egg

1 tablespoon orange juice

Zest of 1 medium orange

½ cup dried cranberries

FOR ICING

2 tablespoons orange juice

1 cup powdered sugar

This mini donut is everything you want for a breakfast treat. With their sweet citrus flavor and surprise burst of tart cranberries, these mini donuts will make you want to open your eyes—and they're the perfect accompaniment to your morning cup of coffee!

1. If using an electric donut maker, preheat according to manufacturer's instructions. If using donut pans, preheat oven to 350°F and grease donut pans.
2. In a small bowl, whisk together milk and sour cream. Set aside. In a separate small bowl, whisk together flour, baking powder, and salt. Set aside.
3. In a large bowl or a stand mixer, cream together butter and sugar until light and fluffy—about 1 minute. Add egg, orange juice, and orange zest. Beat for 30 seconds, scraping down the bowl as needed.
4. Then, alternating flour mixture and milk mixture, combine all ingredients until just blended. Transfer batter to a piping bag, or to a Ziploc bag with the tip cut off.
5. **If using mini-donut pans:** Carefully fill each donut indentation ¾ full. Bake for 7–9 minutes or until a toothpick inserted into a donut comes out clean. Transfer donuts to a cooling rack and cool completely. **If using an electric mini-donut maker:** Carefully fill each donut indentation ¾ full. Bake according to manufacturer's instructions or until a toothpick inserted into a donut comes out clean. Remove donuts from appliance, transfer to a cooling rack, and let cool completely.
6. Place wax paper under a wire rack to collect any drippings for an easy cleanup. Then, in a small bowl, whisk together orange juice and powdered sugar until smooth.
7. Dip the top of each donut into the icing, transfer to a wire rack, and let set for 5 minutes. Serve immediately; donuts can be stored in an airtight container for up to 3 days but are best served fresh.

Blackberry-Sour Cream Mini Donut

 YIELDS 28 MINI DONUTS

FOR DONUTS

2 cups all-purpose flour, sifted

2 teaspoons baking powder

½ teaspoon cinnamon

¼ teaspoon salt

1 large egg

½ cup granulated sugar

¼ cup sour cream

2 tablespoons vegetable oil

1 teaspoon vanilla extract

¾ cup buttermilk

FOR ICING

1½ cups powdered sugar

¼ cup blackberries

Want to give your favorite tangy sour cream mini donut a fun twist? Then this recipe is the one for you. By adding a sweet blackberry frosting, both the look and the flavor of the classic donut change drastically—and get a little fruity!

1. If using an electric donut maker, preheat according to manufacturer's instructions. If using donut pans, preheat oven to 350°F and grease donut pans.
2. In a small bowl, sift together flour, baking powder, cinnamon, and salt. Set aside.
3. In a medium bowl, whisk together egg and sugar. Then add sour cream, oil, and vanilla extract, mixing until thoroughly combined. Gently whisk in the flour mixture, alternating with the buttermilk, until there are no lumps. Transfer batter to a piping bag, or to a Ziploc bag with a hole cut in the tip.
4. **If using mini-donut pans:** Carefully fill each donut indentation ¾ full. Bake for 7–9 minutes or until a toothpick inserted into a donut comes out clean. Transfer donuts to a cooling rack and cool completely. **If using an electric mini-donut maker:** Carefully fill each donut indentation ¾ full. Bake according to manufacturer's instructions or until a toothpick inserted into a donut comes out clean. Remove donuts from appliance, transfer to a cooling rack, and let cool completely.
5. Place wax paper under a wire rack to collect any drippings for an easy cleanup. Then, in a food processor or blender, purée together powdered sugar and blackberries until a smooth icing forms.
6. Dip the top of each donut into the icing, transfer to a wire rack, and let set for 5 minutes. Serve immediately; donuts can be stored in an airtight container for up to 1 day but are best served fresh.

Pineapple Upside-Down Cake Mini Donut

 YIELDS 34 MINI DONUTS

FOR DONUTS

¼ cup unsalted butter

½ cup packed brown sugar

20-ounce can crushed pineapple, drained

1⅓ cups all-purpose flour, sifted

2 teaspoons baking powder

½ teaspoon ground cinnamon

¼ teaspoon salt

1 large egg

½ cup granulated sugar

¾ cup whole milk

3 tablespoons vegetable oil

2 teaspoons vanilla extract

If you're looking for an icing-free mini donut, then this is the recipe for you! Instead of the classic powdered-sugar icing that you might expect, the brown sugar and pineapple found in this recipe pretty much frost these mini donuts all by themselves. Less work simply means more time to enjoy. What could be better?

1. If using an electric donut maker, preheat according to manufacturer's instructions. If using donut pans, preheat oven to 350°F and grease donut pans.
2. In a small saucepan, melt butter and brown sugar over medium heat. Bring to a simmer and cook, stirring constantly, until brown sugar has dissolved. Remove from heat and stir in pineapple. Set aside.
3. In a small bowl, sift together flour, baking powder, cinnamon, and salt. Set aside. In a medium bowl, whisk together egg and sugar. Then add milk, oil, and vanilla extract, mixing until thoroughly combined. Gently stir in the flour mixture, stirring until there are no lumps.
4. **If using mini-donut pans:** Fill the bottom of each donut round with about 1 tablespoon of the pineapple mixture. Then, carefully top pineapple mixture with batter until each donut indentation is ¾ full. Bake for 7–9 minutes or until a toothpick inserted into a donut comes out clean. Transfer donuts to a cooling rack. **If using an electric mini-donut maker:** Fill the bottom of each donut round with about 1 tablespoon of the pineapple mixture. Then, carefully top pineapple mixture with batter until each donut indentation is ¾ full. Bake according to manufacturer's instructions or until a toothpick inserted into a donut comes out clean. Remove donuts from appliance and transfer to a cooling rack.
5. Donuts are best when still warm and do not store well, so serve immediately.

Banana Bread Mini Donut

FOR DONUTS

¾ cup all-purpose flour

1 teaspoon baking powder

½ teaspoon cinnamon

¼ teaspoon salt

½ cup granulated sugar

1 large egg

½ cup mashed banana

¼ cup vegetable oil

1 teaspoon vanilla extract

¼ cup chopped walnuts

FOR ICING

1 tablespoon whole milk

1 teaspoon vanilla extract

1½ cups powdered sugar

½ teaspoon cinnamon

Banana bread is a classic breakfast treat that has been turned into everything from ice cream to truffles, so why not a mini donut, too? With sweet cinnamon in both the icing and the donut, this Banana Bread Mini Donut is sure to make itself at home at your breakfast table!

1. If using an electric donut maker, preheat according to manufacturer's instructions. If using donut pans, preheat oven to 350°F and grease donut pans.
2. In a small bowl, whisk together flour, baking powder, cinnamon, and salt. Set aside.
3. In a medium bowl, whisk together sugar and egg. Then add banana, oil, and vanilla extract, mixing until thoroughly combined. Stir in the flour mixture, stirring until there are no lumps. Gently fold in the walnuts. Transfer batter to a piping bag, or to a Ziploc bag with the tip cut off.
4. **If using mini-donut pans:** Carefully fill each donut indentation ¾ full. Bake for 7–9 minutes or until donuts are slightly browned and spring back when touched. Remove from oven, transfer to a cooling rack, and let cool completely. **If using an electric mini-donut maker:** Carefully fill each donut indentation ¾ full. Bake according to manufacturer's instructions or until the donuts are slightly browned and spring back when touched. Transfer donuts to a cooling rack and let cool completely.
5. Place wax paper under a wire rack to collect any drippings for an easy cleanup. Then, in a small bowl, whisk together milk and vanilla extract. Add powdered sugar and cinnamon, whisking until smooth.
6. Dip the top of each donut into the icing, transfer to a wire rack, and let set for 5 minutes. Serve immediately; donuts can be stored in an airtight container for up to 3 days but are best served fresh.

Banana Bread Mini Donuts

Coconut-Lime Mini Donut

FOR DONUTS

⅔ cup coconut milk

2 tablespoons sour cream

1½ cups all-purpose flour, sifted

1½ teaspoons baking powder

¼ teaspoon salt

6 tablespoons butter, room temperature

½ cup granulated sugar

1 large egg

1 tablespoon lime juice

Zest of 2 limes

FOR ICING

2 tablespoons coconut milk

1½ cups powdered sugar

½ cup shredded coconut

Coconut and lime team together in this mini donut to create a fresh and fruity flavor. Just close your eyes and pretend you are having breakfast at the beach, under bright rays of sunshine. What a way to start the day!

1. If using an electric donut maker, preheat according to manufacturer's instructions. If using donut pans, preheat oven to 350°F and grease donut pans.
2. In a small bowl, whisk together coconut milk and sour cream. Set aside. In a separate small bowl, whisk together flour, baking powder, and salt. Set aside.
3. In a large bowl or a stand mixer, cream together butter and sugar until light and fluffy—about 1 minute. Add egg, lime juice, and lime zest. Beat for 30 seconds, scraping down the bowl as needed.
4. Then, alternating flour mixture and milk mixture, combine all ingredients until just blended. Transfer batter to a piping bag, or to a Ziploc bag with the tip cut off.
5. **If using mini-donut pans:** Carefully fill each donut indentation ¾ full. Bake for 7–9 minutes or until a toothpick inserted into a donut comes out clean. Transfer donuts to a cooling rack and cool completely. **If using an electric mini-donut maker:** Carefully fill each donut indentation ¾ full. Bake according to manufacturer's instructions or until a toothpick inserted into a donut comes out clean. Remove donuts from appliance, transfer to a cooling rack, and let cool completely.
6. Place wax paper under a wire rack to collect any drippings for an easy cleanup. Then, in a small bowl, whisk together coconut milk and powdered sugar until smooth.
7. Dip the top of each donut into the icing and transfer to a wire rack. Sprinkle the tops with the shredded coconut and let set for 5 minutes. Serve immediately; donuts can be stored in an airtight container for up to 2 days but are best served fresh.

Apple Cider Mini Donut

 YIELDS 32 MINI DONUTS

FOR DONUTS

2 cups all-purpose flour, sifted

1½ teaspoons baking powder

1 teaspoon baking soda

2 teaspoons ground cinnamon

¼ teaspoon nutmeg

½ teaspoon salt

1 large egg

½ cup granulated sugar

½ cup applesauce

⅓ cup sour cream

¼ cup vegetable oil

½ cup apple cider

FOR TOPPING

2 teaspoons ground cinnamon

½ cup granulated sugar

3 tablespoons butter, melted

This year, you don't have to go all the way to the orchard to get fresh Apple Cider Mini Donuts. Instead, just pick up a few jugs of fresh apple cider to make your donut dreams come true at home. These tender donuts have the sweet, crisp apple flavor that you love—as well as the spicy cinnamon finish that you crave!

1. If using an electric donut maker, preheat according to manufacturer's instructions. If using donut pans, preheat oven to 350°F and grease donut pans.
2. In a small bowl, sift together flour, baking powder, baking soda, cinnamon, nutmeg, and salt. Set aside.
3. In a medium bowl, whisk together egg and sugar. Then add applesauce, sour cream, and oil, mixing until thoroughly combined. Gently stir in the flour mixture, alternating with the apple cider, stirring until there are no large lumps.
4. **If using mini-donut pans:** Carefully fill each donut indentation ¾ full. Bake for 7–9 minutes or until a toothpick inserted into a donut comes out clean. Transfer donuts to a cooling rack and let cool completely. **If using an electric mini-donut maker:** Carefully fill each donut indentation ¾ full. Bake according to manufacturer's instructions or until a toothpick inserted into a donut comes out clean. Remove donuts from appliance, transfer to a cooling rack, and let cool completely.
5. Toss together cinnamon and sugar in a shallow bowl. While donuts are still hot, quickly dip into the melted butter and coat with the cinnamon-sugar mixture. Donuts are best when still warm and do not store well, so serve immediately.

Clementine Cream Mini Donuts

Clementine Cream Mini Donut

 YIELDS 24 MINI DONUTS

FOR DONUTS

⅔ cup whole milk

2 tablespoons sour cream

1½ cups all-purpose flour, sifted

1½ teaspoons baking powder

¼ teaspoon salt

6 tablespoons butter, room temperature

½ cup granulated sugar

1 large egg

1 tablespoon clementine juice

Zest of 1 large clementine

FOR ICING

1 tablespoon heavy cream

1 tablespoon clementine juice

2 teaspoons clementine zest

1 cup powdered sugar

FOR TOPPING

Zest of 1 clementine, to taste (optional)

Once a year, those darling, little orange clementines appear at the grocery store and give you a reason to celebrate! Now you can use these sweet little citrus bites in a whole new way. These Clementine Cream Mini Donuts have a delicious, light, fresh flavor that can't be beat. Guaranteed!

1. If using an electric donut maker, preheat according to manufacturer's instructions. If using donut pans, preheat oven to 350°F and grease donut pans.
2. In a small bowl, whisk together milk and sour cream. Set aside. In a separate small bowl, whisk together flour, baking powder, and salt. Set aside.
3. In a large bowl or a stand mixer, cream together butter and sugar until light and fluffy— about 1 minute. Add egg, clementine juice, and clementine zest. Beat for 30 seconds, scraping down the bowl as needed.
4. Then, alternating flour mixture and milk mixture, combine all ingredients until just blended. Transfer batter to a piping bag, or to a Ziploc bag with the tip cut off.
5. **If using mini-donut pans:** Carefully fill each donut indentation ¾ full. Bake for 7–9 minutes or until a toothpick inserted into a donut comes out clean. Transfer donuts to a cooling rack and cool completely. **If using an electric mini-donut maker:** Carefully fill each donut indentation ¾ full. Bake according to manufacturer's instructions or until a toothpick inserted into a donut comes out clean. Remove donuts from appliance, transfer to a cooling rack, and let cool completely.
6. Place wax paper under a wire rack to collect any drippings for an easy cleanup. Then, in a small bowl, whisk together cream and clementine juice. Add in clementine zest and powdered sugar, whisking until smooth.
7. Dip the top of each donut into the icing, transfer to a wire rack, and let set for 5 minutes. Sprinkle the tops lightly with clementine zest, if desired. Serve immediately; donuts can be stored in an airtight container for up to 3 days but are best served fresh.

WHEREFORE ART THOU, CLEMENTINE?

When you can't find a darling clementine because they are out of season, don't fret! Instead, try a tangerine, a navel orange, or even a grapefruit.

Cherry Streusel Mini Donut

 YIELDS 28 MINI DONUTS

FOR DONUTS

1¾ cups all-purpose flour, sifted

2 teaspoons baking powder

¼ teaspoon salt

1 large egg

¾ cup granulated sugar

3 tablespoons vegetable oil

¼ cup sour cream

1 teaspoon vanilla extract

½ cup whole milk

½ cup cherry pie filling, chopped

2 tablespoons butter, melted

¼ cup packed brown sugar

¼ cup flour

¼ teaspoon cinnamon

FOR ICING

2 teaspoons whole milk

½ teaspoon vanilla extract

¾ cup powdered sugar

Tender donut, tart cherry pie filling, and a cinnamon-sugar streusel join together to make these Cherry Streusel Mini Donuts outrageously good. For any true cherry fans, add an extra cherry (from the cherry pie filling) to the tops of these mini donuts to really take them to the next level!

1. If using an electric donut maker, preheat according to manufacturer's instructions. If using donut pans, preheat oven to 350°F and grease donut pans.
2. In a small bowl, sift together flour, baking powder, and salt. Set aside.
3. In a medium bowl, whisk together egg and sugar. Then add oil, sour cream, and vanilla extract, mixing until thoroughly combined. Gently stir in the flour mixture, alternating with the milk, stirring until there are no lumps. Carefully fold in the cherry pie filling. Transfer batter to a piping bag, or to a Ziploc bag with a hole cut in the tip.
4. In a small bowl, mix together melted butter, brown sugar, flour, and cinnamon. Fluff with a fork until crumbly.
5. **If using mini-donut pans:** Carefully fill each donut indentation ½ full. Generously sprinkle the tops with the crumbly brown-sugar topping. Bake for 7–9 minutes or until a toothpick inserted into a donut comes out clean. Transfer donuts to a cooling rack and cool completely. **If using an electric mini-donut maker:** Carefully fill each donut indentation ½ full. Generously sprinkle the tops with the crumbly brown-sugar topping. Bake according to manufacturer's instructions or until a toothpick inserted into a donut comes out clean. Remove donuts from appliance, transfer to a cooling rack, and let cool 5 minutes.
6. Place wax paper under a wire rack to collect any drippings for an easy cleanup. Then, in a small bowl, whisk together milk and vanilla extract. Add powdered sugar and whisk until smooth.
7. Drizzle the top of each donut with the icing, transfer to a wire rack, and let set for 5 minutes. Serve immediately, or store in an airtight container for up to 2 days.

Chapter 4

DONUTS OF THE STARS

Call the paparazzi—there's a new star in town! In this chapter, you'll find a star-studded collection of mini donuts that were inspired by your favorite celebrities and their famous food obsessions. Here, you'll find that the red carpet has been rolled out for A-listers ranging from Winnie-the-Pooh and Elvis Presley to Paula Deen and Homer Simpson, the hand-drawn, yellow, bald man who helped donuts first enter the world of pop culture. In the brilliant words of Mr. Simpson, "Mmm, mini donuts." Enjoy!

The Winnie-the-Pooh: Honey-Glazed Fried Mini Donut

 YIELDS 26 MINI DONUTS AND
26 MINI DONUT HOLES

Winnie-the-Pooh was always getting himself in trouble on his hunts for some sweet, sticky honey. After taking one bite of these fabulous raised donuts with a creamy honey glaze, you will be right there next to him, stuck at the bottom of a honey pot!

FOR DONUTS

2 tablespoons water, warmed

1.25-ounce envelope fast rise yeast

¾ cup whole milk, warmed

¼ cup granulated sugar

½ teaspoon salt

1 large egg

3 tablespoons shortening or lard

2½ cups all-purpose flour

Vegetable oil or peanut oil, for frying

FOR ICING

3 tablespoons honey

1 tablespoon whole milk

1½ cups powdered sugar

1. In the bowl of your stand mixer, with the paddle attachment (or in a large bowl if you are going to knead the dough by hand), whisk together warm water and yeast and let stand for 5 minutes.
2. Add milk, sugar, salt, egg, shortening, and 1 cup of flour. Mix on medium-low for 2 minutes, then switch to the dough hook. Slowly add the remaining 1½ cups flour, ½ cup at a time. Once you have added all the flour, knead on medium for 2–3 minutes, until dough no longer sticks to the bowl. Turn up the speed to medium-high, and continue to knead dough for 3–4 minutes, until dough is smooth.
3. Transfer dough to a greased bowl, and cover with a slightly damp tea towel. Place bowl in a warm area (or in an oven preheated to 200°F and then turned off) for about 1 hour. Dough is ready when it has doubled in size.
4. Transfer raised dough to a lightly floured surface, and carefully roll out until it is ½" thick. Cut out doughnuts with a floured 2" biscuit cutter, and then cut out the center of each donut with a floured 1" biscuit cutter.
5. Place donuts and donut holes on a lightly floured cookie sheet, and cover again with a slightly damp tea towel. Place in a warm area (or in an oven preheated to 200°F and then turned off) for about 1 hour. Dough is ready when it has doubled in size.
6. Heat oil in a large, deep skillet or a deep fryer to 350°F.
7. Once oil is hot, working with 4 to 6 donuts at a time, carefully drop donuts into oil. Fry for 1–2 minutes or until golden brown; flip each donut and fry the other side.
8. Remove and drain on a plate lined with newspaper or paper towels. Continue this process until each donut has been fried.
9. Place wax paper under a wire rack to collect any drippings for an easy cleanup. Then, in a small bowl, whisk together honey, milk, and powdered sugar, whisking until smooth.
10. While the donuts are still warm, dip the top of each donut and donut hole into the icing, transfer to a wire rack, and let set for 5 minutes. Serve immediately; donuts can be stored in an airtight container for up to 3 days but are best served while still warm.

The Elvis:
Peanut Butter and Banana Mini Donut

 YIELDS 18 MINI DONUTS

FOR DONUTS

¾ cup all-purpose flour

1 teaspoon baking powder

½ teaspoon cinnamon

¼ teaspoon salt

½ cup granulated sugar

1 large egg

½ cup mashed banana

¼ cup vegetable oil

1 teaspoon vanilla extract

FOR FROSTING

2 tablespoons creamy peanut butter

½ cup powdered sugar

1 tablespoon whole milk

Elvis's love of fried peanut-butter-and-banana sandwiches is as famous as his hips. Well, almost. This recipe gives you a dense banana mini donut with creamy peanut butter frosting, all in honor of the King. Elvis would have loved it!

1. If using an electric donut maker, preheat according to manufacturer's instructions. If using donut pans, preheat oven to 350°F and grease donut pans.

2. In a small bowl, whisk together flour, baking powder, cinnamon, and salt. Set aside.

3. In a medium bowl, whisk together sugar and egg. Then add banana, oil, and vanilla extract, mixing until thoroughly combined. Stir in the flour mixture, stirring until there are no lumps. Transfer batter to a piping bag, or to a Ziploc bag with the tip cut off.

4. **If using mini-donut pans:** Carefully fill each donut indentation ¾ full. Bake for 7–9 minutes or until donuts are slightly browned and spring back when touched. Remove from oven, transfer to a cooling rack, and let cool completely. **If using an electric mini-donut maker:** Carefully fill each donut indentation ¾ full. Bake according to manufacturer's instructions or until the donuts are slightly browned and spring back when touched. Transfer donuts to a cooling rack and let cool completely.

5. Place wax paper under a wire rack to collect any drippings for an easy cleanup. Then, in a small bowl, whisk together peanut butter and powdered sugar. Slowly add milk, whisking constantly until you get a smooth frosting.

6. Dip the top of each donut into the frosting and transfer to a wire rack. Let frosting set for 10 minutes and then serve. Donuts can be stored in an airtight container for up to 2 days but are best when eaten fresh.

The Kenan and Kel: Orange Soda Mini Donut

 YIELDS 24 MINI DONUTS

FOR DONUTS

1⅓ cups all-purpose flour, sifted

2 teaspoons baking powder

¼ teaspoon salt

1 large egg

½ cup granulated sugar

¾ cup orange soda

¼ cup vegetable oil

½ teaspoon orange extract

FOR ICING

1½ cups powdered sugar

1½ tablespoons orange soda

Kenan and Kel ruled Nickelodeon, starting with the show All That *and ending up with their own show,* Kenan & Kel. *Every '90s kid remembers Kenan and Kel and their infamous obsession with orange soda, which means that the only way to properly honor them is with an Orange Soda Mini Donut!*

1. If using an electric donut maker, preheat according to manufacturer's instructions. If using donut pans, preheat oven to 350°F and grease donut pans.
2. In a small bowl, sift together flour, baking powder, and salt. Set aside.
3. In a medium bowl, whisk together egg and sugar. Then add orange soda, oil, and orange extract, mixing until thoroughly combined. Gently stir in the flour mixture, stirring until there are no lumps.
4. **If using mini-donut pans:** Carefully fill each donut indentation ¾ full. Bake for 7–9 minutes or until a toothpick inserted into a donut comes out clean. Transfer donuts to a cooling rack and cool completely. **If using an electric mini-donut maker:** Carefully fill each donut indentation ¾ full. Bake according to manufacturer's instructions or until a toothpick inserted into a donut comes out clean. Remove donuts from appliance, transfer to a cooling rack, and let cool completely.
5. Place wax paper under a wire rack to collect any drippings for an easy cleanup. Then, in a small bowl, whisk together powdered sugar and orange soda until smooth.
6. Dip the top of each donut into the icing, transfer to a wire rack, and let set for 5 minutes. Serve immediately; donuts can be stored in an airtight container for up to 2 days but are best served fresh.

SODA POP

If you're not a fan of orange soda, feel free to substitute any of your favorite carbonated beverages to make these mini donuts. The recipe is delicious with anything from grape soda to Dr Pepper. Just be sure to remove the orange extract.

The Kenan and Kel: Orange Soda Mini Donuts

The President Jimmy Carter: Peanut Crunch Mini Donut

 YIELDS 30 MINI DONUTS

FOR DONUTS

1 cup all-purpose flour

2 teaspoons baking powder

¼ teaspoon salt

½ cup granulated sugar

¼ cup creamy peanut butter

1 large egg

¾ cup whole milk

2 tablespoons vegetable oil

FOR FROSTING

2 tablespoons creamy peanut butter

½ cup powdered sugar

1 tablespoon whole milk

FOR TOPPING

½ cup chopped lightly salted, roasted peanuts

Jimmy Carter is well known for his unusual job as a peanut farmer before he became president of the United States. Although you may think he was nuts, he probably just dreamed of having a peanut crunch donut named after him. From one goober lover to another, these donuts are for you, Jimmy!

1. If using an electric donut maker, preheat according to manufacturer's instructions. If using donut pans, preheat oven to 350°F and grease donut pans.
2. In a small bowl, whisk together flour, baking powder, and salt. Set aside.
3. In a medium bowl, cream together sugar and peanut butter until light and fluffy. Carefully add egg, milk, and oil, mixing until thoroughly combined. Then, alternating the flour mixture and milk mixture, combine all ingredients until there are no lumps.
4. **If using mini-donut pans:** Carefully fill each donut indentation ¾ full. Bake for 7–9 minutes or until donuts are slightly browned and spring back when touched. Remove from oven, transfer to a cooling rack, and let cool completely. **If using an electric mini-donut maker:** Carefully fill each donut indentation ¾ full. Bake according to manufacturer's instructions or until the donuts are slightly browned and spring back when touched. Transfer donuts to a cooling rack and let cool completely.
5. Place wax paper under a wire rack to collect any drippings for an easy cleanup. Then, in a small bowl, whisk together peanut butter and powdered sugar. Slowly add milk, whisking constantly until you get a smooth frosting.
6. Dip the top of each donut into the frosting and transfer to a wire rack. Immediately sprinkle the top of each donut with chopped peanuts. Let frosting set for 5 minutes and then serve. Donuts can be stored in an airtight container for up to 2 days but are best when eaten fresh.

IT'S SALTY, BABY

By using peanuts that have been lightly salted, you get that awesome salty-sweet combination that everyone loves. Just be sure the peanuts are *lightly* salted . . . otherwise, your donuts will end up tasting like a salt lick.

The President Jimmy Carter: Peanut Crunch Mini Donuts

The Curious George:
Banana Cream Mini Donut

 YIELDS 18 MINI DONUTS

FOR DONUTS

¾ cup all-purpose flour

1 teaspoon baking powder

½ teaspoon cinnamon

¼ teaspoon salt

½ cup granulated sugar

1 large egg

½ cup mashed banana

¼ cup vegetable oil

1 tablespoon heavy cream

1 teaspoon vanilla extract

FOR ICING

2 tablespoons heavy cream

1 teaspoon vanilla extract

1½ cups powdered sugar

Curious George was onto something when he was eating all those bananas: Not only are they loaded with potassium and good for you, but they make a great mini donut, too. Curious George is often seen with a big smile on his face and a banana in his hand, but imagine how much happier he would be with a Banana Cream Mini Donut instead!

1. If using an electric donut maker, preheat according to manufacturer's instructions. If using donut pans, preheat oven to 350°F and grease donut pans.
2. In a small bowl, whisk together flour, baking powder, cinnamon, and salt. Set aside.
3. In a medium bowl, whisk together sugar and egg. Then add banana, oil, heavy cream, and vanilla extract, mixing until thoroughly combined. Stir in the flour mixture, stirring until there are no lumps. Transfer batter to a piping bag, or to a Ziploc bag with the tip cut off.
4. **If using mini-donut pans:** Carefully fill each donut indentation ¾ full. Bake for 7–9 minutes or until donuts are slightly browned and spring back when touched. Remove from oven, transfer to a cooling rack, and let cool completely. **If using an electric mini-donut maker:** Carefully fill each donut indentation ¾ full. Bake according to manufacturer's instructions or until the donuts are slightly browned and spring back when touched. Transfer donuts to a cooling rack and let cool completely.
5. Place wax paper under a wire rack to collect any drippings for an easy cleanup. Then, in a small bowl, whisk together heavy cream and vanilla extract. Add powdered sugar, whisking until smooth.
6. Dip the top of each donut into the icing, transfer to a wire rack, and let set for 10 minutes. Serve immediately, or store in an airtight container in the refrigerator for up to 3 days.

The Paula Deen: Butter Cake Mini Donut

 YIELDS 34 MINI DONUTS

FOR DONUTS

½ cup (1 stick) unsalted butter, melted

18.25-ounce box yellow cake mix

2 large eggs

¼ cup sour cream

1 teaspoon vanilla extract

FOR TOPPING

½ cup powdered sugar

If you look up Paula Deen in the dictionary, there are no words. Instead, there is a large photo of gloriously yellow butter. In her honor, here is a Butter Cake Mini Donut that only a true Paula Deen fan could appreciate.

1. If using an electric donut maker, preheat according to manufacturer's instructions. If using donut pans, preheat oven to 350°F and grease donut pans.
2. In a large bowl, cream together melted butter and yellow cake mix. Add eggs, sour cream, and vanilla extract, mixing until smooth.
3. **If using mini-donut pans:** Carefully fill each donut indentation ¾ full. Bake for 7–9 minutes or until a toothpick inserted into a donut comes out clean. Transfer donuts to a cooling rack and cool for 5 minutes. **If using an electric mini-donut maker:** Carefully fill each donut indentation ¾ full. Bake according to manufacturer's instructions or until a toothpick inserted into a donut comes out clean. Remove donuts from appliance, transfer to a cooling rack, and cool for 5 minutes.
4. Once donuts are no longer hot to the touch, place powdered sugar into a brown paper bag or a Ziploc bag. Working with 2 or 3 donuts at a time, shake to coat with powdered sugar. Serve immediately, or store in an airtight container for up to 3 days.

The Bugs Bunny: Carrot Cake Mini Donut

 YIELDS 24 MINI DONUTS

FOR DONUTS

⅔ cup whole milk

2 tablespoons sour cream

1½ cups all-purpose flour, sifted

1½ teaspoons baking powder

½ teaspoon ground cinnamon

¼ teaspoon salt

6 tablespoons butter, room temperature

½ cup granulated sugar

1 large egg

2 teaspoons vanilla extract

½ cup grated carrots

¼ cup golden raisins, chopped

FOR FROSTING

2 ounces cream cheese, softened

1 cup powdered sugar

½ teaspoon ground cinnamon

1 tablespoon whole milk

Excuse the pun, but these mini donuts are worth their weight in gold . . . 24 carrot gold, that is. Bugs Bunny would be happy to trade in his standard carrot for one of these Carrot Cake Mini Donuts—and so will you!

1. If using an electric donut maker, preheat according to manufacturer's instructions. If using donut pans, preheat oven to 350°F and grease donut pans.
2. In a small bowl, whisk together milk and sour cream. Set aside. In a separate small bowl, whisk together flour, baking powder, cinnamon, and salt. Set aside.
3. In a large bowl or a stand mixer, cream together butter and sugar until light and fluffy— about 1 minute. Add egg and vanilla extract. Beat for 30 seconds, scraping down the bowl as needed.
4. Then, alternating flour mixture and milk mixture, combine all ingredients until just blended. Gently stir in carrots and golden raisins. Transfer batter to a piping bag, or to a Ziploc bag with the tip cut off.
5. **If using mini-donut pans:** Carefully fill each donut indentation ¾ full. Bake for 7–9 minutes or until a toothpick inserted into a donut comes out clean. Transfer donuts to a cooling rack and cool completely. **If using an electric mini-donut maker:** Carefully fill each donut indentation ¾ full. Bake according to manufacturer's instructions or until a toothpick inserted into a donut comes out clean. Remove donuts from appliance, transfer to a cooling rack, and let cool completely.
6. Place wax paper under a wire rack to collect any drippings for an easy cleanup. Then, in a stand mixer, blend together cream cheese, powdered sugar, and cinnamon. Slowly add milk, whisking constantly, until you get a smooth frosting.
7. Dip the top of each donut into the frosting and transfer to a wire rack. Let frosting set for 5 minutes and then serve. Donuts can be stored in an airtight container in the refrigerator for up to 2 days but are best when eaten fresh.

The Homer Simpson: Pink-Sprinkle Mini Donut

 YIELDS 30 MINI DONUTS

FOR DONUTS

1⅓ cups all-purpose flour, sifted

2 teaspoons baking powder

¼ teaspoon salt

1 large egg

½ cup granulated sugar

¾ cup whole milk

3 tablespoons vegetable oil

2 teaspoons vanilla extract

FOR ICING

1 tablespoon whole milk

1 teaspoon vanilla extract

1½ cups powdered sugar

2–3 drops red food coloring

FOR TOPPING

2 ounces multicolored sprinkles

"'Dear Homer, IOU one emergency donut. Signed, Homer.' Bastard! He's always one step ahead." —Homer Simpson. Homer has always known the importance of a good donut, and now that you're making a mini version of his favorite, there'll be plenty to go around!

1. If using an electric donut maker, preheat according to manufacturer's instructions. If using donut pans, preheat oven to 350°F and grease donut pans.
2. In a small bowl, sift together flour, baking powder, and salt. Set aside.
3. In a medium bowl, whisk together egg and sugar. Then add milk, oil, and vanilla extract, mixing until thoroughly combined. Gently stir in the flour mixture, stirring until there are no lumps.
4. **If using mini-donut pans:** Carefully fill each donut indentation ¾ full. Bake for 7–9 minutes or until a toothpick inserted into a donut comes out clean. Transfer donuts to a cooling rack and cool completely. **If using an electric mini-donut maker:** Carefully fill each donut indentation ¾ full. Bake according to manufacturer's instructions or until a toothpick inserted into a donut comes out clean. Remove donuts from appliance, transfer to a cooling rack, and let cool completely.
5. Place wax paper under a wire rack to collect any drippings for an easy cleanup. Then, in a small bowl, whisk together milk and vanilla extract. Add powdered sugar, whisking until smooth. Add red food coloring 1 drop at a time, until you reach the desired pink color.
6. Dip the top of each donut into the icing and transfer to a wire rack. Immediately garnish the tops with the multicolored sprinkles and let set for 5 minutes. Donuts can be stored in an airtight container for up to 3 days but are best served fresh.

The Homer Simpson: Pink-Sprinkle Mini Donuts

The Cookie Monster: Cookie Dough Mini Donut

 YIELDS 28 MINI DONUTS

Is there anything better than raw cookie dough? No! So what better way to honor Sesame Street's Cookie Monster than to top a mini donut with delicious, eggless cookie-dough balls? It's completely safe and totally scrumdiddlyumptious! The Cookie Monster would definitely approve.

FOR DONUTS

1⅓ cups all-purpose flour, sifted

2 teaspoons baking powder

¼ teaspoon salt

1 large egg

½ cup granulated sugar

¾ cup whole milk

3 tablespoons vegetable oil

2 teaspoons vanilla extract

FOR COOKIE DOUGH

6 tablespoons butter, room temperature

⅓ cup packed brown sugar

⅓ cup granulated sugar

½ teaspoon vanilla extract

2 tablespoons whole milk

1 cup all-purpose flour

½ teaspoon salt

¼ cup mini chocolate chips

FOR ICING

4 tablespoons butter

2 tablespoons whole milk

1 tablespoon light corn syrup

2 ounces bittersweet chocolate, roughly chopped

1 cup powdered sugar, sifted

1. If using an electric donut maker, preheat according to manufacturer's instructions. If using donut pans, preheat oven to 350°F and grease donut pans.
2. In a small bowl, sift together flour, baking powder, and salt. Set aside.
3. In a medium bowl, whisk together egg and sugar. Then add milk, oil, and vanilla extract, mixing until thoroughly combined. Gently stir in the flour mixture, stirring until there are no lumps.
4. **If using mini-donut pans:** Carefully fill each donut indentation ¾ full. Bake for 7–9 minutes or until a toothpick inserted into a donut comes out clean. Transfer donuts to a cooling rack and cool completely. **If using an electric mini-donut maker:** Carefully fill each donut indentation ¾ full. Bake according to manufacturer's instructions or until a toothpick inserted into a donut comes out clean. Remove donuts from appliance, transfer to a cooling rack, and let cool completely.
5. In a medium bowl, cream together butter, brown sugar, and granulated sugar. Add vanilla extract and milk. Stir in flour and salt, mixing until incorporated. Gently stir in chocolate chips. Using ½ teaspoon as your measuring guide, roll small balls of cookie dough. Set aside.
6. Place wax paper under a wire rack to collect any drippings for an easy cleanup. Then, in a small saucepan over medium heat, melt butter. Add milk, corn syrup, and chopped chocolate, stirring slowly to allow chocolate to melt completely.
7. Once melted, remove from heat and whisk in powdered sugar. Immediately dip the top of each donut into the icing, and transfer to a wire rack.
8. Top frosting with cookie-dough balls, let icing set for 10 minutes, and then serve. Donuts are best when eaten fresh.

Chapter 5

BAKERY SPECIALS

There are few sights more beautiful than that glowing neon sign reading "Hot Now" in the window of your local bakery. We all know what that sign means: fresh, hot donuts! Instead of the traditional donut flavors, all of the donuts that you'll find in this chapter were inspired by the cakes, pies, and cookies found in your local bakery. With flavors ranging from the Samoa Mini Donut, inspired by the famous Girl Scout cookie, to the delicious Strawberry Shortcake Mini Donut with real whipped cream, you'll soon find yourself saying goodbye to your baker, because these mini donuts are here to stay. So grab a number, step up to the counter, and find out which Bakery Special mini donut is for you!

Dulce de Leche Mini Donut

 YIELDS 30 MINI DONUTS

FOR DONUTS

1⅓ cups all-purpose flour, sifted

2 teaspoons baking powder

½ teaspoon cinnamon

¼ teaspoon salt

1 large egg

½ cup granulated sugar

¾ cup whole milk

3 tablespoons vegetable oil

2 teaspoons vanilla extract

FOR TOPPING

1 5-ounce can dulce de leche

When translated directly into English, dulce de leche means "candy of milk." With its thick, spreadable texture and almost caramel-like flavor, dulce de leche is exactly what you'd imagine milk candy would taste like. While it is perfect when eaten with a spoon, dulce de leche makes one heck of a donut, too. Enjoy!

1. If using an electric donut maker, preheat according to manufacturer's instructions. If using donut pans, preheat oven to 350°F and grease donut pans.
2. In a small bowl, sift together flour, baking powder, cinnamon, and salt. Set aside.
3. In a medium bowl, whisk together egg and sugar. Then add milk, oil, and vanilla extract, mixing until thoroughly combined. Gently stir in the flour mixture, stirring until there are no lumps.
4. **If using mini-donut pans:** Carefully fill each donut indentation ¾ full. Bake for 7–9 minutes or until a toothpick inserted into a donut comes out clean. Transfer donuts to a cooling rack.
   If using an electric mini-donut maker: Carefully fill each donut indentation ¾ full. Bake according to manufacturer's instructions or until a toothpick inserted into a donut comes out clean. Remove donuts from appliance and transfer to a cooling rack.
5. Spread the top of each donut with the dulce de leche and serve immediately. Donuts can be stored in an airtight container for up to 3 days but are best served fresh.

MAKE YOUR OWN

Instead of buying a can of pre-made dulce de leche, you can make your own. Using a large saucepan, completely submerge a 14-ounce can of sweetened condensed milk in water. Bring water to a slow simmer, and continue to simmer for 3½ hours, adding more water as needed. Let can cool before opening, then enjoy. Tip: Be sure to keep can completely submerged in water the entire time. If not, the can may explode because of the heat.

Dulce de Leche Mini Donut

Salted Caramel Mini Donut

FOR DONUTS

1⅓ cups all-purpose flour, sifted

2 teaspoons baking powder

¼ teaspoon salt

1 large egg

½ cup packed brown sugar

¾ cup whole milk

3 tablespoons vegetable oil

2 teaspoons vanilla extract

FOR CARAMEL SAUCE

16 squares of caramel, unwrapped

1 tablespoon milk

FOR TOPPING

Flaky sea salt, to taste

There are few things that the dessert-loving community reveres as highly as the combination of salty and sweet. In fact, salted caramels are quickly becoming a popular treat in candy stores around the nation. Because of this passion, when making a Caramel Mini Donut, there seems to be only one option . . . add sea salt!

1. If using an electric donut maker, preheat according to manufacturer's instructions. If using donut pans, preheat oven to 350°F and grease donut pans.
2. In a small bowl, sift together flour, baking powder, and salt. Set aside.
3. In a medium bowl, whisk together egg and brown sugar. Then add milk, oil, and vanilla extract, mixing until thoroughly combined. Gently stir in the flour mixture, stirring until there are no lumps.
4. **If using mini-donut pans:** Carefully fill each donut indentation ¾ full. Bake for 7–9 minutes or until a toothpick inserted into a donut comes out clean. Transfer donuts to a cooling rack and let cool completely. **If using an electric mini-donut maker:** Carefully fill each donut indentation ¾ full. Bake according to manufacturer's instructions or until a toothpick inserted into a donut comes out clean. Remove donuts from appliance and transfer to a cooling rack and let cool completely.
5. Place wax paper under a wire rack to collect any drippings for an easy cleanup. Then, in a large, microwave-safe bowl, melt caramel and milk in 15-second increments, stirring after each, until you get a smooth texture. Dip the top of each mini donut in the melted caramel, and sprinkle the top with a little flaky sea salt.
6. Let donuts set for 5 minutes and then serve. Donuts can be stored in an airtight container for up to 3 days but are best served fresh.

Salted Caramel Mini Donut

Marble Cake Mini Donut

 YIELDS 30 MINI DONUTS

FOR DONUTS

1⅓ cups all-purpose flour, sifted

2 teaspoons baking powder

¼ teaspoon salt

1 large egg

½ cup granulated sugar

¾ cup whole milk

3 tablespoons vegetable oil

2 teaspoons vanilla extract

2 tablespoons cocoa powder, sifted

FOR ICING

1 tablespoon whole milk

1 teaspoon vanilla extract

1½ cups powdered sugar

Marble cake is traditionally found at birthday parties, but now you can serve it up at the breakfast table. And, although this swirled combination of vanilla and chocolate donut batter looks impressive, it's thankfully easy to make. Wow your guests with your amazing kitchen skills by making these Marble Cake Mini Donuts!

1. If using an electric donut maker, preheat according to manufacturer's instructions. If using donut pans, preheat oven to 350°F and grease donut pans.
2. In a small bowl, sift together flour, baking powder, and salt. Set aside.
3. In a medium bowl, whisk together egg and sugar. Then add milk, oil, and vanilla extract, mixing until thoroughly combined. Gently stir in the flour mixture, stirring until there are no lumps.
4. Divide batter between two bowls, and in one of the bowls, whisk in the cocoa powder. This way you will have one bowl of chocolate batter and one bowl of vanilla batter. Then, in a measuring cup (with a spout) or a batter dispenser, pour a small layer of the vanilla batter, followed by a layer of the chocolate batter. Repeat this process until all of the batter has been layered.
5. **If using mini-donut pans:** Carefully fill each donut indentation ¾ full. Bake for 7–9 minutes or until a toothpick inserted into a donut comes out clean. Transfer donuts to a cooling rack and cool completely. **If using an electric mini-donut maker:** Carefully fill each donut indentation ¾ full. Bake according to manufacturer's instructions or until a toothpick inserted into a donut comes out clean. Remove donuts from appliance, transfer to a cooling rack, and let cool completely.
6. Place wax paper under a wire rack to collect any drippings for an easy cleanup. Then, in a small bowl, whisk together milk and vanilla extract. Add powdered sugar, whisking until smooth.
7. Dip the top of each donut into the icing, transfer to a wire rack, and let set for 5 minutes. Serve immediately; donuts can be stored in an airtight container for up to 3 days but are best served fresh.

Cinnamon-Marshmallow Fluff Mini Donut

FOR DONUTS

1⅓ cups all-purpose flour, sifted

2 teaspoons baking powder

1 teaspoon ground cinnamon

¼ teaspoon salt

1 large egg

½ cup granulated sugar

¾ cup whole milk

3 tablespoons vegetable oil

2 teaspoons vanilla extract

FOR ICING

½ cup Marshmallow Fluff

The combination of delicate cinnamon and sweet marshmallow fluff gives these donuts a light and fun feel. By using already-prepared Marshmallow Fluff as the icing, you save a lot of preparation time, which makes these mini donuts perfect for busy mornings!

1. If using an electric donut maker, preheat according to manufacturer's instructions. If using donut pans, preheat oven to 350°F and grease donut pans.
2. In a small bowl, sift together flour, baking powder, cinnamon, and salt. Set aside.
3. In a medium bowl, whisk together egg and sugar. Then add milk, oil, and vanilla extract, mixing until thoroughly combined. Gently stir in the flour mixture, stirring until there are no lumps.
4. **If using mini-donut pans:** Carefully fill each donut indentation ¾ full. Bake for 7–9 minutes or until a toothpick inserted into a donut comes out clean. Transfer donuts to a cooling rack and cool for 5 minutes. **If using an electric mini-donut maker:** Carefully fill each donut indentation ¾ full. Bake according to manufacturer's instructions or until a toothpick inserted into a donut comes out clean. Remove donuts from appliance, transfer to a cooling rack, and cool for 5 minutes.
5. While donuts are still warm to the touch, coat the tops with a healthy smear of Marshmallow Fluff. These donuts are best while still warm, so serve immediately.

Samoa Mini Donuts

Samoa Mini Donut

 YIELDS 30 MINI DONUTS

FOR DONUTS

1 cup all-purpose flour, sifted

¼ cup cocoa powder, sifted

2 teaspoons baking powder

¼ teaspoon salt

1 large egg

½ cup granulated sugar

¾ cup whole milk

3 tablespoons vegetable oil

1 teaspoon vanilla extract

FOR ICING

4 tablespoons butter

2 tablespoons whole milk

1 tablespoon light corn syrup

2 ounces bittersweet chocolate, roughly chopped

1 cup powdered sugar, sifted

FOR TOPPING

1 cup sweetened shredded coconut

½ cup Smucker's caramel-flavored Sundae Syrup

It's cruel and unusual punishment to have to wait a full year for the Girl Scouts to sell delicious Samoa cookies again. The good news is that the amazing combination of chocolate, caramel, and coconut found in this recipe is sure to fill the void where those Samoa cookies used to be!

1. If using an electric donut maker, preheat according to manufacturer's instructions. If using donut pans, preheat oven to 350°F and grease donut pans.
2. In a small bowl, sift together flour, cocoa powder, baking powder, and salt. Set aside.
3. In a medium bowl, whisk together egg and sugar. Then add milk, oil, and vanilla extract, mixing until thoroughly combined. Gently stir in the flour mixture, stirring until there are no lumps.
4. **If using mini-donut pans:** Carefully fill each donut indentation ¾ full. Bake for 7–9 minutes or until a toothpick inserted in a donut comes out clean. Transfer donuts to a cooling rack and let cool completely. **If using an electric mini-donut maker:** Carefully fill each donut indentation ¾ full. Bake according to manufacturer's instructions or until a toothpick inserted into a donut comes out clean. Remove donuts from appliance, transfer to a cooling rack, and let cool completely.
5. Place wax paper under a wire rack to collect any drippings for an easy cleanup. Then, in a small saucepan over medium heat, melt butter. Add milk, corn syrup, and chopped chocolate, stirring slowly to allow chocolate to melt completely.
6. Once melted, remove from heat and whisk in powdered sugar. Immediately dip the top of each donut into the icing and transfer to a wire rack.
7. Sprinkle the top of each donut with coconut and let set for 10 minutes. Then, drizzle the top of each donut with Smucker's caramel-flavored Sundae Syrup and serve immediately. These donuts do not store well and should be eaten fresh.

Gingerbread Mini Donut

 YIELDS 18 MINI DONUTS

FOR DONUTS

1⅓ cups all-purpose flour, sifted

2 teaspoons baking powder

1 teaspoon cinnamon

½ teaspoon ginger

Pinch of allspice

¼ teaspoon salt

1 large egg

⅓ cup packed brown sugar

2 tablespoons pure maple syrup

1 tablespoon sour cream

¼ cup vegetable oil

½ cup whole milk

FOR ICING

3 tablespoons butter

⅓ cup packed brown sugar

3 tablespoons whole milk

¾ cup powdered sugar

Gingerbread always brings back warm memories of cold fall nights, but that doesn't mean you should only have it once a year. These Gingerbread Mini Donuts are made with brown sugar, maple syrup, and all of your favorite fall spices. Be a daredevil and try them in the spring instead!

1. If using an electric donut maker, preheat according to manufacturer's instructions. If using donut pans, preheat oven to 350°F and grease donut pans.
2. In a small bowl, sift together flour, baking powder, cinnamon, ginger, allspice, and salt. Set aside.
3. In a medium bowl, whisk together egg and brown sugar. Then add maple syrup, sour cream, oil, and milk, mixing until thoroughly combined. Gently stir in the flour mixture, stirring until there are no lumps.
4. **If using mini-donut pans:** Carefully fill each donut indentation ¾ full. Bake for 7–9 minutes or until a toothpick inserted into a donut comes out clean. Transfer donuts to a cooling rack and cool completely. **If using an electric mini-donut maker:** Carefully fill each donut indentation ¾ full. Bake according to manufacturer's instructions or until a toothpick inserted into a donut comes out clean. Remove donuts from appliance, transfer to a cooling rack, and let cool completely.
5. Place wax paper under a wire rack to collect any drippings for an easy cleanup. Then, in a small saucepan over medium heat, melt butter. Add brown sugar and milk, stirring slowly to allow sugar to melt completely.
6. Once melted, remove from heat and whisk in powdered sugar. Immediately dip the top of each donut into the icing and transfer to a wire rack.
7. Let frosting set for 10 minutes and then serve. Donuts can be stored in an airtight container for up to 2 days but are best when eaten fresh.

Butterscotch-Banana Mini Donut

 YIELDS 18 MINI DONUTS

FOR DONUTS

¾ cup all-purpose flour

1 teaspoon baking powder

½ teaspoon cinnamon

¼ teaspoon salt

½ cup granulated sugar

1 large egg

½ cup mashed banana

¼ cup vegetable oil

1 teaspoon vanilla extract

FOR BUTTERSCOTCH GLAZE

¾ cup butterscotch morsels

1 tablespoon whole milk

The combination of butterscotch and banana is a new fad that's making its way onto bakery shelves. With the distinctive banana and creamy, traditional butterscotch flavors, these mini donuts are sure to become a new favorite!

1. If using an electric donut maker, preheat according to manufacturer's instructions. If using donut pans, preheat oven to 350°F and grease donut pans.
2. In a small bowl, whisk together flour, baking powder, cinnamon, and salt. Set aside.
3. In a medium bowl, whisk together sugar and egg. Then add banana, oil, and vanilla extract, mixing until thoroughly combined. Stir in the flour mixture, stirring until there are no lumps. Transfer batter to a piping bag, or to a Ziploc bag with the tip cut off.
4. **If using mini-donut pans:** Carefully fill each donut indentation ¾ full. Bake for 7–9 minutes or until donuts are slightly browned and spring back when touched. Remove from oven, transfer to a cooling rack, and let cool completely. **If using an electric mini-donut maker:** Carefully fill each donut indentation ¾ full. Bake according to manufacturer's instructions or until the donuts are slightly browned and spring back when touched. Transfer donuts to a cooling rack and let cool completely.
5. Place wax paper under a wire rack to collect any drippings for an easy cleanup. Then, in a small, microwave-safe bowl, microwave the butterscotch morsels and milk in 15-second increments, stirring each time. Once you reach a smooth, lump-free butterscotch glaze, let sit and cool for 2 minutes.
6. Dip the top of each donut into the glaze, transfer to a wire rack, and let set for 5 minutes. Serve immediately, or store in an airtight container for up to 3 days.

Snickerdoodle Fried Mini Donut

 YIELDS 26 MINI DONUTS AND
26 MINI DONUT HOLES

FOR DONUTS

2 tablespoons water, warmed

1.25-ounce envelope fast-rise yeast

¾ cup whole milk, warmed

¼ cup granulated sugar

1 teaspoon cream of tartar

½ teaspoon salt

1 large egg

3 tablespoons shortening or lard

2½ cups all-purpose flour

Vegetable oil or peanut oil, for frying

FOR TOPPING

2 teaspoons ground cinnamon

½ cup granulated sugar

With their tangy, cinnamon-sugar flavor, snickerdoodles are a favorite cookie all across the U.S. of A. To achieve that bakery-fresh flavor in a mini donut, add a few pinches of cream of tartar to the dough, and shake those hot fried mini donuts in some sparkling cinnamon sugar! Voilà, Snickerdoodle Fried Mini Donuts!

1. In the bowl of your stand mixer, with the paddle attachment (or in a large bowl if you are going to knead the dough by hand), whisk together warm water and yeast and let stand for 5 minutes.
2. Add milk, sugar, cream of tartar, salt, egg, shortening, and 1 cup of flour. Mix on medium-low for 2 minutes, then switch to the dough hook. Slowly add the remaining 1½ cups flour, ½ cup at a time. Once you have added all the flour, knead on medium for 2–3 minutes, until dough no longer sticks to the bowl. Turn up the speed to medium-high, and continue to knead dough for 3–4 minutes, until dough is smooth.
3. Transfer dough to a greased bowl, and cover with a slightly damp tea towel. Place bowl in a warm area (or in an oven preheated to 200°F and then turned off) for about 1 hour. Dough is ready when it has doubled in size.
4. Transfer raised dough to a lightly floured surface and carefully roll out until it is ½" thick. Cut out doughnuts with a floured 2" biscuit cutter, and then cut out the center of each donut with a floured 1" biscuit cutter.
5. Place donuts and donut holes on a lightly floured cookie sheet, and cover again with a slightly damp tea towel. Place in a warm area (or in an oven preheated to 200°F and then turned off) for about 1 hour. Dough is ready when it has doubled in size.
6. Heat oil in a large, deep skillet or a deep fryer to 350°F.
7. Once oil is hot, working with 4 to 6 donuts at a time, carefully drop donuts into oil. Fry for 1–2 minutes or until golden brown; flip each donut and fry the other side.
8. Remove and drain on a plate lined with newspaper or paper towels. Continue this process until each donut has been fried.
9. Place cinnamon and sugar in a large brown paper bag and shake to combine. While donuts are still hot, quickly toss mini donuts in the cinnamon-sugar mixture, 4 to 5 at a time. Donuts are best when still warm and do not store well, so serve immediately.

Strawberry Shortcake Mini Donut

 YIELDS 24 MINI DONUTS

FOR DONUTS

⅔ cup whole milk

2 tablespoons sour cream

1½ cups all-purpose flour, sifted

1½ teaspoons baking powder

¼ teaspoon salt

6 tablespoons butter, room temperature

½ cup granulated sugar

1 large egg

2 teaspoons vanilla extract

FOR TOPPING

16 large strawberries, sliced

FOR WHIPPED CREAM

¾ cup heavy whipping cream

1 teaspoon vanilla extract

3 tablespoons powdered sugar

Early each spring, grocery stores fill with beautiful ripe strawberries ready to be taken home. This year, instead of a traditional strawberry shortcake, try out these adorable Strawberry Shortcake Mini Donuts for a new twist on a bakery favorite!

1. If using an electric donut maker, preheat according to manufacturer's instructions. If using donut pans, preheat oven to 350°F and grease donut pans.
2. In a small bowl, whisk together milk and sour cream. Set aside. In a separate small bowl, whisk together flour, baking powder, and salt. Set aside.
3. In a large bowl or a stand mixer, cream together butter and sugar until light and fluffy—about 1 minute. Add egg and vanilla extract. Beat for 30 seconds, scraping down the bowl as needed.
4. Then, alternating flour mixture and milk mixture, combine all ingredients until just blended. Transfer batter to a piping bag, or to a Ziploc bag with the tip cut off.
5. **If using mini-donut pans:** Carefully fill each donut indentation ¾ full. Bake for 7–9 minutes or until a toothpick inserted into a donut comes out clean. Transfer donuts to a cooling rack and cool completely. **If using an electric mini-donut maker:** Carefully fill each donut indentation ¾ full. Bake according to manufacturer's instructions or until a toothpick inserted into a donut comes out clean. Remove donuts from appliance, transfer to a cooling rack, and let cool completely.
6. Once the donuts are cooled, slice in half. On one half of each donut, layer 3 or 4 slices of strawberries. In a stand mixer, whip cream until peaks are just starting to form. Add vanilla extract and powdered sugar, and continue beating until stiff peaks form. Transfer whipped cream to a piping bag, and pipe on top of the strawberry layer.
7. Sandwich each mini donut together with the remaining donut half and serve immediately. These donuts do not store well and so should be eaten fresh.

Sweet Potato–Marshmallow Mini Donut

 YIELDS 28 MINI DONUTS

FOR DONUTS

1¾ cups all-purpose flour, sifted

2 teaspoons baking powder

1 teaspoon cinnamon

¼ teaspoon nutmeg

¼ teaspoon ginger

¼ teaspoon salt

1 large egg

½ cup granulated sugar

¾ cup sweet potato purée

¼ tablespoon vegetable oil

1 teaspoon vanilla extract

½ cup whole milk

FOR TOPPING

½ cup Marshmallow Fluff

You know—and love—the delicious sweet-potato casserole that graces your Thanksgiving table. But just try to imagine it in mini-donut form. With a tender sweet-potato base and a sticky Marshmallow Fluff topping, you'll want to give thanks for these Sweet Potato–Marshmallow Mini Donuts!

1. If using an electric donut maker, preheat according to manufacturer's instructions. If using donut pans, preheat oven to 350°F and grease donut pans.
2. In a small bowl, sift together flour, baking powder, cinnamon, nutmeg, ginger, and salt. Set aside.
3. In a medium bowl, whisk together egg and sugar. Then add sweet potato purée, oil, and vanilla extract, mixing until thoroughly combined. Gently whisk in the flour mixture, alternating with the milk, until there are no lumps. Transfer batter to a piping bag, or to a Ziploc bag with a hole cut in the tip.
4. **If using mini-donut pans:** Carefully fill each donut indentation ¾ full. Bake for 7–9 minutes or until a toothpick inserted into a donut comes out clean. Transfer donuts to a cooling rack and cool for 5 minutes. **If using an electric mini-donut maker:** Carefully fill each donut indentation ¾ full. Bake according to manufacturer's instructions or until a toothpick inserted into a donut comes out clean. Remove donuts from appliance, transfer to a cooling rack, and let cool for 5 minutes.
5. While the donuts are still warm to the touch, frost the top of each donut with a healthy smear of Marshmallow Fluff. These donuts are best served while still warm, so serve immediately.

Brown Butter Mini Donut

 YIELDS 24 MINI DONUTS

FOR DONUTS

⅔ cup whole milk

2 tablespoons sour cream

1½ cups all-purpose flour, sifted

1½ teaspoons baking powder

¼ teaspoon salt

½ cup granulated sugar

6 tablespoons browned butter, cooled (see sidebar for instructions)

1 large egg

2 teaspoons vanilla extract

FOR ICING

1½ tablespoons whole milk

1 teaspoon vanilla extract

1½ cups powdered sugar

When you cook butter until it turns a dark, golden brown, it takes on a whole new flavor profile. The butter that you previously knew is gone, and in its place is a rich, nutty sauce. When added to baked goods, brown butter takes them to a whole new depth . . . which is exactly what it does for these Brown Butter Mini Donuts!

1. If using an electric donut maker, preheat according to manufacturer's instructions. If using donut pans, preheat oven to 350°F and grease donut pans.
2. In a small bowl, whisk together milk and sour cream. Set aside. In a separate small bowl, whisk together flour, baking powder, and salt. Set aside.
3. In large bowl, cream together cooled browned butter and sugar. Add egg and vanilla extract. Then, alternating flour mixture and milk mixture, combine all ingredients until just blended. Transfer batter to a piping bag, or to a Ziploc bag with the tip cut off.
4. **If using mini-donut pans:** Carefully fill each donut indentation ¾ full. Bake for 7–9 minutes or until a toothpick inserted into a donut comes out clean. Transfer donuts to a cooling rack and cool completely. **If using an electric mini-donut maker:** Carefully fill each donut indentation ¾ full. Bake according to manufacturer's instructions or until a toothpick inserted into a donut comes out clean. Remove donuts from appliance, transfer to a cooling rack, and let cool completely.
5. Place wax paper under a wire rack to collect any drippings for an easy cleanup. Then, in a small bowl, whisk together milk, vanilla extract, and powdered sugar until smooth.
6. Dip the top of each donut into the icing, transfer to a wire rack, and let set for 5 minutes. Serve immediately; donuts can be stored in an airtight container for up to 1 day but are best served fresh.

BROWNED BUTTER HOW-TO

Melt butter in a small saucepan over medium heat. Cook, swirling pan occasionally, until butter turns a deep golden color and you see dark flecks, about 10 minutes. Transfer to a bowl and let cool until no longer warm to the touch, about 20 minutes.

Cinnamon-Raisin Mini Donut

FOR DONUTS

1⅓ cups all-purpose flour, sifted

2 teaspoons baking powder

1 teaspoon ground cinnamon

¼ teaspoon salt

1 large egg

½ cup granulated sugar

¾ cup whole milk

3 tablespoons vegetable oil

2 teaspoons vanilla extract

¼ cup raisins

FOR ICING

1 tablespoon whole milk

1 teaspoon vanilla extract

¼ teaspoon ground cinnamon

1½ cups powdered sugar

Swirls of cinnamon and hidden raisins make cinnamon-raisin bread a classic at the breakfast table. But a tender, moist donut, scented with cinnamon and filled with raisins, is the perfect substitute. Enjoy!

1. If using an electric donut maker, preheat according to manufacturer's instructions. If using donut pans, preheat oven to 350°F and grease donut pans.
2. In a small bowl, sift together flour, baking powder, cinnamon, and salt. Set aside.
3. In a medium bowl, whisk together egg and sugar. Then add milk, oil, and vanilla extract, mixing until thoroughly combined. Gently stir in the flour mixture, stirring until there are no lumps. Once smooth, gently fold in the raisins until thoroughly combined.
4. **If using mini-donut pans:** Carefully fill each donut indentation ¾ full. Bake for 7–9 minutes or until a toothpick inserted into a donut comes out clean. Transfer donuts to a cooling rack and let cool completely. **If using an electric mini-donut maker:** Carefully fill each donut indentation ¾ full. Bake according to manufacturer's instructions or until a toothpick inserted into a donut comes out clean. Remove donuts from appliance, transfer to a cooling rack, and let cool completely.
5. Place wax paper under a wire rack to collect any drippings for an easy cleanup. Then, in a small bowl, whisk together milk and vanilla extract. Add cinnamon and powdered sugar, whisking until smooth.
6. Dip the top of each donut into the icing and transfer to a wire rack. Let icing set for 5 minutes, and then re-dip the top of each donut. Let set for 5 more minutes and then serve. Donuts can be stored in an airtight container for up to 3 days but are best when served fresh.

Cinnamon-Raisin Mini Donuts

Pumpkin Spice with Cinnamon-Maple Glaze Mini Donut

 YIELDS 28 MINI DONUTS

FOR DONUTS

1¾ cups all-purpose flour, sifted

2 teaspoons baking powder

1 teaspoon cinnamon

¼ teaspoon nutmeg

¼ teaspoon ginger

¼ teaspoon salt

1 large egg

½ cup granulated sugar

¾ cup canned pumpkin purée

¼ cup vegetable oil

1 teaspoon vanilla extract

½ cup whole milk

1½ cups powdered sugar

½ teaspoon cinnamon

FOR ICING

½ teaspoon whole milk

2 tablespoons pure maple syrup

¼ teaspoon maple extract

1½ cups powdered sugar

When the weather starts to turn colder, and the leaves begin to fall from the trees, there is only one mini donut that will do: a Pumpkin Spice with Cinnamon-Maple Glaze. These mini donuts truly encompass everything that is fall.

1. If using an electric donut maker, preheat according to manufacturer's instructions. If using donut pans, preheat oven to 350°F and grease donut pans.

2. In a small bowl, sift together flour, baking powder, cinnamon, nutmeg, ginger, and salt. Set aside.

3. In a medium bowl, whisk together egg and sugar. Then add pumpkin purée, oil, and vanilla extract, mixing until thoroughly combined. Gently whisk in the flour mixture, alternating with the milk, until there are no lumps. Transfer batter to a piping bag, or to a Ziploc bag with a hole cut in the tip.

4. **If using mini-donut pans:** Carefully fill each donut indentation ¾ full. Bake for 7–9 minutes or until a toothpick inserted into a donut comes out clean. Transfer donuts to a cooling rack and cool completely. **If using an electric mini-donut maker:** Carefully fill each donut indentation ¾ full. Bake according to manufacturer's instructions or until a toothpick inserted into a donut comes out clean. Remove donuts from appliance, transfer to a cooling rack, and let cool completely.

5. Place wax paper under a wire rack to collect any drippings for an easy cleanup. Then, in a small bowl, whisk together milk, pure maple syrup, and maple extract. Add powdered sugar, whisking until smooth.

6. Dip the top of each donut into the icing, transfer to a wire rack, and let set for 5 minutes. Serve immediately, or store in an airtight container for up to 3 days.

Chapter 6

CANDY-AISLE DONUTS

We all have been there. You know, that embarrassing moment when you catch yourself drooling at the shelves of brightly wrapped candies in the candy aisle? Well, thanks to the recipes found in this chapter, you have a better excuse to buy all those mountains of candy. Just think of it as your golden ticket to the mini-donut candy factory! Here, you'll learn that melting down a Milky Way can create one hell of a frosting, that chocolate malted milk isn't just for kids, and that pretzels and caramel simply belong on top of a mini donut. So wipe off those chocolate-coated fingers, and turn the page to begin your candy-aisle journey!

Snickers Mini Donut

 YIELDS 30 MINI DONUTS

While they say a Snickers satisfies, a Snickers Mini Donut truly satisfies. These tender chocolate mini donuts have a sweet drizzle of caramel running through the center, as well as a coating of caramel on top. They're a total win-win!

FOR DONUTS

1 cup all-purpose flour, sifted

⅓ cup cocoa powder, sifted

2 teaspoons baking powder

¼ teaspoon salt

1 large egg

½ cup granulated sugar

¾ cup whole milk

2 tablespoons vegetable oil

2 tablespoons sour cream

½ teaspoon vanilla extract

¼ cup Smucker's caramel-flavored Sundae Syrup

FOR ICING

4 tablespoons butter

2 tablespoons whole milk

1 tablespoon light corn syrup

2 ounces bittersweet chocolate, roughly chopped

FOR TOPPING

¼ cup Smucker's caramel-flavored Sundae Syrup

1 Snickers, chopped

1. If using an electric donut maker, preheat according to manufacturer's instructions. If using donut pans, preheat oven to 350°F and grease donut pans.
2. In a small bowl, sift together flour, cocoa powder, baking powder, and salt. Set aside.
3. In a medium bowl, whisk together egg and sugar. Then add milk, oil, sour cream, and vanilla extract, mixing until thoroughly combined. Gently stir in the flour mixture, stirring until there are no lumps.
4. **If using mini-donut pans:** Carefully fill each donut indentation ¾ full. Drizzle a small circle of Smucker's caramel-flavored Sundae Syrup on each donut. Bake for 7–9 minutes or until a toothpick inserted into a donut comes out clean. Transfer donuts to a cooling rack and let cool completely. **If using an electric mini-donut maker:** Carefully fill each donut indentation ¾ full. Drizzle a small circle of Smucker's caramel-flavored Sundae Syrup on each donut. Bake according to manufacturer's instructions or until a toothpick inserted into a donut comes out clean. Remove donuts from appliance, transfer to a cooling rack, and let cool completely.
5. Place wax paper under a wire rack to collect any drippings for an easy cleanup. Then, in a small saucepan over medium heat, melt butter. Add milk, corn syrup, and chopped chocolate, stirring slowly to allow chocolate to melt completely.
6. Once melted, remove from heat and whisk in powdered sugar. Immediately dip the top of each donut into the icing and then transfer to a wire rack and let cool for 10 minutes.
7. Place remaining Smucker's caramel-flavored Sundae Syrup in a small bowl. Dip the top of each donut into the caramel syrup and sprinkle the top of each donut with chopped Snickers. These donuts do not store well, so serve immediately.

Snickers Mini Donuts

Chocolate-Heath Bar Crunch Mini Donut

 YIELDS 30 MINI DONUTS

FOR DONUTS

1 cup all-purpose flour, sifted

⅓ cup cocoa powder, sifted

2 teaspoons baking powder

¼ teaspoon salt

1 large egg

½ cup granulated sugar

¾ cup whole milk

2 tablespoons vegetable oil

2 tablespoons sour cream

½ teaspoon vanilla extract

FOR FROSTING

4 tablespoons butter

2 tablespoons whole milk

1 tablespoon light corn syrup

2 ounces bittersweet chocolate, roughly chopped

1 cup powdered sugar, sifted

FOR TOPPING

1 Heath Bar, chopped

For some silly reason, Heath bars are one of the most overlooked candy bars in the candy aisle. But that's all about to change. With their smooth milk chocolate outside and crunchy toffee inside, they sure do make one outrageous donut!

1. If using an electric donut maker, preheat according to manufacturer's instructions. If using donut pans, preheat oven to 350°F and grease donut pans.
2. In a small bowl, sift together flour, cocoa powder, baking powder, and salt. Set aside.
3. In a medium bowl, whisk together egg and sugar. Then add milk, oil, sour cream, and vanilla extract, mixing until thoroughly combined. Gently stir in the flour mixture, stirring until there are no lumps.
4. **If using mini-donut pans:** Carefully fill each donut indentation ¾ full. Bake for 7–9 minutes or until a toothpick inserted into a donut comes out clean. Transfer donuts to a cooling rack and let cool completely. **If using an electric mini-donut maker:** Carefully fill each donut indentation ¾ full. Bake according to manufacturer's instructions or until a toothpick inserted into a donut comes out clean. Remove donuts from appliance, transfer to a cooling rack, and let cool completely.
5. Place wax paper under a wire rack to collect any drippings for an easy cleanup. Then, in a small saucepan over medium heat, melt butter. Add milk, corn syrup, and chopped chocolate, stirring slowly to allow chocolate to melt completely.
6. Once melted, remove from heat and whisk in powdered sugar. Immediately dip the top of each donut into the frosting and transfer to a wire rack.
7. Sprinkle the top of each donut with chopped Heath Bar. Let frosting set for 10 minutes and then serve. Donuts can be stored in an airtight container for up to 2 days but are best when eaten fresh.

Chocolate-Heath Bar Crunch Mini Donuts

Reese's Peanut Butter Cup Mini Donut

 YIELDS 30 MINI DONUTS

FOR DONUTS

1 cup all-purpose flour

2 teaspoons baking powder

¼ teaspoon salt

½ cup granulated sugar

¼ cup creamy peanut butter

1 large egg

¾ cup whole milk

2 tablespoons vegetable oil

FOR ICING

4 tablespoons butter

2 tablespoons whole milk

1 tablespoon light corn syrup

2 ounces bittersweet chocolate, roughly chopped

1 cup powdered sugar, sifted

FOR TOPPING

2 Reese's Peanut Butter Cups, chopped

Reese's Peanut Butter Cups will always be one of America's favorite candies because of their delicious combination of creamy peanut butter and milk chocolate. What better way to celebrate those flavors than in donut form? This recipe starts with a fluffy peanut butter donut and is followed by a layer of rich chocolate icing that is then topped with beautiful chopped Reese's Peanut Butter Cups. Perfection!

1. If using an electric donut maker, preheat according to manufacturer's instructions. If using donut pans, preheat oven to 350°F and grease donut pans.
2. In a small bowl, whisk together flour, baking powder, and salt. Set aside.
3. In a medium bowl, cream together sugar and peanut butter until light and fluffy. Carefully add egg, milk, and oil, mixing until thoroughly combined. Then, alternating the flour mixture and milk mixture, combine all ingredients until there are no lumps.
4. **If using mini-donut pans:** Carefully fill each donut indentation ¾ full. Bake for 7–9 minutes or until donuts are slightly browned and spring back when touched. Remove from oven, transfer to a cooling rack, and let cool completely. **If using an electric mini-donut maker:** Carefully fill each donut indentation ¾ full. Bake according to manufacturer's instructions or until the donuts are slightly browned and spring back when touched. Transfer donuts to a cooling rack and let cool completely.
5. Place wax paper under a wire rack to collect any drippings for an easy cleanup. Then, in a small saucepan over medium heat, melt butter. Add milk, corn syrup, and chopped chocolate, stirring slowly to allow chocolate to melt completely.
6. Once melted, remove from heat and whisk in powdered sugar. Immediately dip the top of each donut into the icing and transfer to a wire rack.
7. Sprinkle the top of each donut with chopped Reese's Peanut Butter Cups. Let icing set for 10 minutes and then serve. Donuts can be stored in an airtight container for up to 2 days but are best when eaten fresh.

Nestlé Crunch Mini Donut

 YIELDS 30 MINI DONUTS

FOR DONUTS

1 cup all-purpose flour, sifted

⅓ cup cocoa powder, sifted

2 teaspoons baking powder

¼ teaspoon salt

1 large egg

½ cup granulated sugar

¾ cup whole milk

2 tablespoons vegetable oil

2 tablespoons sour cream

½ teaspoon vanilla extract

2 Nestlé Crunch bars, chopped and divided

FOR ICING

4 tablespoons butter

2 tablespoons whole milk

1 tablespoon light corn syrup

2 ounces bittersweet chocolate, roughly chopped

1 cup powdered sugar, sifted

This donut is the crispy dream of every Nestlé Crunch fan out there. This mini donut uses chopped up Nestlé Crunch on both the inside and the top, making it the best way to highlight this classic crispy candy bar!

1. If using an electric donut maker, preheat according to manufacturer's instructions. If using donut pans, preheat oven to 350°F and grease donut pans.

2. In a small bowl, sift together flour, cocoa powder, baking powder, and salt. Set aside.

3. In a medium bowl, whisk together egg and sugar. Then add milk, oil, sour cream, and vanilla extract, mixing until thoroughly combined. Gently stir in the flour mixture, stirring until there are no lumps. Then, gently stir in half of the chopped Nestlé Crunch bar.

4. **If using mini-donut pans:** Carefully fill each donut indentation ¾ full. Bake for 7–9 minutes or until a toothpick inserted into a donut comes out clean. Transfer donuts to a cooling rack and let cool completely. **If using an electric mini-donut maker:** Carefully fill each donut indentation ¾ full. Bake according to manufacturer's instructions or until a toothpick inserted into a donut comes out clean. Remove donuts from appliance, transfer to a cooling rack, and let cool completely.

5. Place wax paper under a wire rack to collect any drippings for an easy cleanup. Then, in a small saucepan over medium heat, melt butter. Add milk, corn syrup, and chopped chocolate, stirring slowly to allow chocolate to melt completely.

6. Once melted, remove from heat and whisk in powdered sugar. Immediately dip the top of each donut into the icing and transfer to a wire rack.

7. Sprinkle the top of each donut with the remaining chopped Nestlé Crunch bar. Let icing set for 10 minutes and then serve. Donuts can be stored in an airtight container for up to 2 days but are best when eaten fresh.

*Caramel Turtle
Mini Donuts*

Caramel Turtle Mini Donut

 YIELDS 30 MINI DONUTS

FOR DONUTS

1 cup all-purpose flour, sifted

⅓ cup cocoa powder, sifted

2 teaspoons baking powder

¼ teaspoon salt

1 large egg

½ cup granulated sugar

¾ cup whole milk

2 tablespoons vegetable oil

2 tablespoons sour cream

½ teaspoon vanilla extract

FOR CARAMEL SAUCE

16 caramel squares, unwrapped

2 teaspoons whole milk

FOR TOPPING

⅓ cup finely chopped pretzels

Turtles aren't just for Valentine's Day anymore! By taking a chocolate donut and adding sweet caramel and salty pretzels, you can have them in mini-donut form any day of the year. Talk about true love!

1. If using an electric donut maker, preheat according to manufacturer's instructions. If using donut pans, preheat oven to 350°F and grease donut pans.
2. In a small bowl, sift together flour, cocoa powder, baking powder, and salt. Set aside.
3. In a medium bowl, whisk together egg and sugar. Then add milk, oil, sour cream, and vanilla extract, mixing until thoroughly combined. Gently stir in the flour mixture, stirring until there are no lumps.
4. **If using mini-donut pans:** Carefully fill each donut indentation ¾ full. Bake for 7–9 minutes or until a toothpick inserted into a donut comes out clean. Transfer donuts to a cooling rack and let cool completely. **If using an electric mini-donut maker:** Carefully fill each donut indentation ¾ full. Bake according to manufacturer's instructions or until a toothpick inserted into a donut comes out clean. Remove donuts from appliance, transfer to a cooling rack, and let cool completely.
5. Place wax paper under a wire rack to collect any drippings for an easy cleanup. In a small, microwave-safe bowl, place caramel squares and milk. Microwave on high, stirring every 15 seconds, until smooth. Dip the top of each donut into the caramel and transfer to a wire rack.
6. Immediately sprinkle the top of each donut with chopped pretzels. These donuts do not store well, so serve immediately.

Chocolate-Andes Mint Mini Donut

 YIELDS 30 MINI DONUTS

FOR DONUTS

1 cup all-purpose flour, sifted

⅓ cup cocoa powder, sifted

2 teaspoons baking powder

¼ teaspoon salt

1 large egg

½ cup granulated sugar

½ cup whole milk

2 tablespoons vegetable oil

2 tablespoons sour cream

1 teaspoon crème de menthe

FOR ICING

4 tablespoons butter, softened

1 cup powdered sugar

2 tablespoons crème de menthe

½ teaspoon vanilla extract

NOT FOR THE KIDS' TABLE

Crème de menthe is a mint-flavored liqueur that is made by steeping dried peppermint leaves in grain alcohol. It can be found at your local liquor store and comes in both green and clear (pick whichever color you like better, it does not change the taste). To use up leftover crème de menthe, purée with vanilla ice cream to make a delicious adult milkshake!

To create the perfect mint-and-chocolate combination that you find in an Andes Crème de Menthe candy, these mini donuts use crème de menthe. If you are a hardcore fan, top these with chopped Andes mints, but be careful not to let your donuts get too minty (if that's possible!).

1. If using an electric donut maker, preheat according to manufacturer's instructions. If using donut pans, preheat oven to 350°F and grease donut pans.
2. In a small bowl, sift together flour, cocoa powder, baking powder, and salt. Set aside.
3. In a medium bowl, whisk together egg and sugar. Then add milk, oil, sour cream, and crème de menthe, mixing until thoroughly combined. Gently stir in the flour mixture, stirring until there are no lumps.
4. **If using mini-donut pans:** Carefully fill each donut indentation ¾ full. Bake for 7–9 minutes or until a toothpick inserted into a donut comes out clean. Transfer donuts to a cooling rack and let cool completely. **If using an electric mini-donut maker:** Carefully fill each donut indentation ¾ full. Bake according to manufacturer's instructions or until a toothpick inserted into a donut comes out clean. Remove donuts from appliance, transfer to a cooling rack, and let cool completely.
5. Place wax paper under a wire rack to collect any drippings for an easy cleanup. Then, in stand mixer, beat together butter and powdered sugar, scraping down the sides as needed. Add in crème de menthe and vanilla extract, mixing until smooth.
6. Ice the top of each donut with crème de menthe icing and then serve. Donuts can be stored in an airtight container for up to 3 days.

Milky Way Mini Donut

 YIELDS 30 MINI DONUTS

FOR DONUTS

1 cup all-purpose flour, sifted

¼ cup chocolate malted-milk powder

2 tablespoons cocoa powder, sifted

2 teaspoons baking powder

¼ teaspoon salt

1 large egg

½ cup granulated sugar

¾ cup whole milk

2 tablespoons vegetable oil

2 tablespoons sour cream

½ teaspoon vanilla extract

FOR ICING

2 tablespoons butter

2 teaspoons whole milk

2 (2.05-ounce) Milky Way bars, chopped

1 cup powdered sugar

Traditionally, nougat is a candy prepared with nuts, but the nougat inside a Milky Way contains no nuts. So, as with the rule-breaking Milky Way candies, these mini donuts are full of chocolate malted-milk flavor . . . without those pesky nuts!

1. If using an electric donut maker, preheat according to manufacturer's instructions. If using donut pans, preheat oven to 350°F and grease donut pans.
2. In a small bowl, sift together flour, malted-milk powder, cocoa powder, baking powder, and salt. Set aside.
3. In a medium bowl, whisk together egg and sugar. Then add milk, oil, sour cream, and vanilla extract, mixing until thoroughly combined. Gently stir in the flour mixture, stirring until there are no lumps.
4. **If using mini-donut pans:** Carefully fill each donut indentation ¾ full. Bake for 7–9 minutes or until a toothpick inserted into a donut comes out clean. Transfer donuts to a cooling rack and let cool completely. **If using an electric mini-donut maker:** Carefully fill each donut indentation ¾ full. Bake according to manufacturer's instructions or until a toothpick inserted into a donut comes out clean. Remove donuts from appliance, transfer to a cooling rack, and let cool completely.
5. Place wax paper under a wire rack to collect any drippings for an easy cleanup. Then, in a small saucepan over medium heat, melt butter. Add milk and chopped Milky Way bars, stirring slowly to allow chocolate to melt completely.
6. Once melted, remove from heat and whisk in powdered sugar. Immediately dip the top of each donut into the icing and transfer to a wire rack.
7. Let icing set for 10 minutes and then serve. Donuts can be stored in an airtight container for up to 2 days but are best when eaten fresh.

Butterfinger Mini Donut

 YIELDS 30 MINI DONUTS

FOR DONUTS

1⅓ cups all-purpose flour, sifted

2 teaspoons baking powder

¼ teaspoon salt

1 large egg

½ cup granulated sugar

¾ cup whole milk

3 tablespoons vegetable oil

2 teaspoons vanilla extract

FOR FROSTING

2 ounces cream cheese, softened

½ cup powdered sugar

⅓ cup Cool Whip

FOR TOPPING

1 2.1-ounce Butterfinger bar, chopped

By combining Cool Whip and cream cheese, you have the perfect Butterfinger frosting to sit on top of a dense chocolate mini donut. These mini donuts are so good that you'll be telling everyone to keep their hands off your Butterfinger!

1. If using an electric donut maker, preheat according to manufacturer's instructions. If using donut pans, preheat oven to 350°F and grease donut pans.
2. In a small bowl, sift together flour, baking powder, and salt. Set aside.
3. In a medium bowl, whisk together egg and sugar. Then add milk, oil, and vanilla extract, mixing until thoroughly combined. Gently stir in the flour mixture, stirring until there are no lumps.
4. **If using mini-donut pans:** Carefully fill each donut indentation ¾ full. Bake for 7–9 minutes or until a toothpick inserted into a donut comes out clean. Transfer donuts to a cooling rack and cool completely. **If using an electric mini-donut maker:** Carefully fill each donut indentation ¾ full. Bake according to manufacturer's instructions or until a toothpick inserted into a donut comes out clean. Remove donuts from appliance, transfer to a cooling rack, and let cool completely.
5. In stand mixer, beat cream cheese and powdered sugar until smooth. Add Cool Whip and half of the chopped Butterfinger bar, mixing until combined. Top each mini donut with a healthy smear of frosting, and then sprinkle with the remaining chopped Butterfinger.
6. Serve donuts immediately. Donuts may be stored in an airtight container in the refrigerator for up to 2 days but are best when eaten fresh.

Butterfinger Mini Donut

100 Grand Fried Mini Donut

 YIELDS 26 MINI DONUTS

Break open these warm, chocolate yeast donuts and you'll find a delicious mix of melted chocolate, caramel, and 100 Grand candy bar. It's almost as good as actually finding a 100 grand in cash inside! Maybe even better . . .

FOR DONUTS

2¼ cups all-purpose flour

¼ cup cocoa powder

2 tablespoons water, warmed

1.25-ounce envelope fast-rise yeast

¾ cup whole milk, warmed

¼ cup granulated sugar

½ teaspoon salt

1 large egg

3 tablespoons shortening or lard

Vegetable oil or peanut oil, for frying

13 fun-size 100 Grand bars, cut in half

FOR ICING

2 tablespoons whole milk

1 teaspoon vanilla extract

1½ cups powdered sugar

1. In a medium bowl, sift together flour and cocoa powder and set aside. In the bowl of your stand mixer, with the paddle attachment (or in a large bowl if you are going to knead the dough by hand), whisk together warm water and yeast and let stand for 5 minutes.
2. Add milk, sugar, salt, egg, shortening, and 1 cup of flour mixture. Mix on medium-low for 2 minutes, then switch to the dough hook. Slowly add the remaining 1½ cups flour mixture, ½ cup at a time. Once you have added all the flour mixture, knead on medium for 2–3 minutes, until dough no longer sticks to the bowl. Turn up the speed to medium-high, and continue to knead dough for 3–4 minutes, until dough is smooth.
3. Transfer dough to a greased bowl, and cover with a slightly damp tea towel. Place bowl in a warm area (or in an oven preheated to 200°F and then turned off) for about 1 hour. Dough is ready when it has doubled in size.
4. Transfer raised dough to a lightly floured surface and carefully roll out until it is ½" thick. Cut out doughnuts with a floured 2" biscuit cutter.
5. Place donuts on a lightly floured cookie sheet, and cover again with a slightly damp tea towel. Place in a warm area (or in an oven preheated to 200°F and then turned off) for about 1 hour. Dough is ready when it has doubled in size.
6. Heat oil in a large, deep skillet or a deep fryer to 350°F.
7. While the oil is heating, use a sharp knife to cut a small slit in the side of each donut. Gently press one piece of the 100 Grand into the center of the mini donut. Seal the edge shut by slightly pinching the dough with your fingers.
8. Once oil is hot, working with 4 to 6 donuts at a time, carefully drop donuts into oil. Fry for 1–2 minutes or until golden brown; flip each donut and fry the other side.
9. Remove and drain on a plate lined with newspaper or paper towels. Continue this process until each donut has been fried.
10. Place wax paper under a wire rack to collect any drippings for an easy cleanup. Then, in a small bowl, whisk together milk and vanilla extract. Add powdered sugar, whisking until smooth.
11. While still warm, dip the top of each donut and donut hole into the icing, transfer to a wire rack, and let set for 5 minutes. Serve immediately; because of the melted chocolate candy bar inside, these mini donuts are best served fresh.

Chocolate-Almond Bar Mini Donut

 YIELDS 30 MINI DONUTS

FOR DONUTS

1 cup all-purpose flour, sifted

⅓ cup cocoa powder, sifted

2 teaspoons baking powder

¼ teaspoon salt

1 large egg

½ cup granulated sugar

¾ cup whole milk

2 tablespoons vegetable oil

2 tablespoons sour cream

1 teaspoon almond extract

FOR ICING

4 tablespoons butter

2 tablespoons whole milk

1 tablespoon light corn syrup

2 ounces bittersweet chocolate, roughly chopped

1 cup powdered sugar, sifted

FOR TOPPING

1 Hershey's Milk Chocolate Bar with Almonds, chopped

SUGARY SUBSTITUTIONS

Don't worry if you forgot to grab a Hershey's Milk Chocolate Bar with Almonds! Instead, just chop up some plain almonds and sprinkle them on top. With the chocolate icing and chocolate donut, a little extra chocolate won't be missed.

Chocolate and almonds have been paired together in desserts and chocolate candy bars forever. It even seems as though the crunchy bites of nutty almonds and the smooth chocolate are destined to be together. With just a small splash of almond extract, these mini donuts really set themselves apart!

1. If using an electric donut maker, preheat according to manufacturer's instructions. If using donut pans, preheat oven to 350°F and grease donut pans.
2. In a small bowl, sift together flour, cocoa powder, baking powder, and salt. Set aside.
3. In a medium bowl, whisk together egg and sugar. Then add milk, oil, sour cream, and almond extract, mixing until thoroughly combined. Gently stir in the flour mixture, stirring until there are no lumps.
4. **If using mini-donut pans:** Carefully fill each donut indentation ¾ full. Bake for 7–9 minutes or until a toothpick inserted into a donut comes out clean. Transfer donuts to a cooling rack and let cool completely. **If using an electric mini-donut maker:** Carefully fill each donut indentation ¾ full. Bake according to manufacturer's instructions or until a toothpick inserted into a donut comes out clean. Remove donuts from appliance, transfer to a cooling rack, and let cool completely.
5. Place wax paper under a wire rack to collect any drippings for an easy cleanup. Then, in a small saucepan over medium heat, melt butter. Add milk, corn syrup, and chopped chocolate, stirring slowly to allow chocolate to melt completely.
6. Once melted, remove from heat and whisk in powdered sugar. Immediately dip the top of each donut into the icing and transfer to a wire rack.
7. Sprinkle the top of each donut with chopped Hershey's Milk Chocolate Bar with Almonds. Let frosting set for 10 minutes and then serve. Donuts can be stored in an airtight container for up to 2 days but are best when eaten fresh.

Whopper Malted Chocolate Mini Donuts

Whopper Malted Chocolate Mini Donut

 YIELDS 30 MINI DONUTS

FOR DONUTS

1 cup all-purpose flour, sifted

¼ cup chocolate malted-milk powder

2 tablespoons cocoa powder, sifted

2 teaspoons baking powder

¼ teaspoon salt

1 large egg

½ cup granulated sugar

¾ cup whole milk

2 tablespoons vegetable oil

2 tablespoons sour cream

½ teaspoon vanilla extract

FOR ICING

4 tablespoons butter

2 tablespoons whole milk

1 tablespoon light corn syrup

2 ounces bittersweet chocolate, roughly chopped

1 cup powdered sugar, sifted

FOR TOPPING

½ cup Whoppers, chopped

....

WHAT IS CHOCOLATE MALTED-MILK POWDER?

Malted-milk powder was originally sold as an infant formula, but these days, it is most commonly found in the center of Whoppers. You can find this ingredient in your local grocery store, next to the hot chocolate or other powdered drinks.

The secret to these moist chocolate donuts is swapping some of the cocoa powder for malted milk. Between the density of flavors in the donut, the thick chocolate icing, and the chopped Whoppers, these mini donuts are simply little bombs of chocolate-y goodness!

1. If using an electric donut maker, preheat according to manufacturer's instructions. If using donut pans, preheat oven to 350°F and grease donut pans.

2. In a small bowl, sift together flour, malted-milk powder, cocoa powder, baking powder, and salt. Set aside.

3. In a medium bowl, whisk together egg and sugar. Then add milk, oil, sour cream, and vanilla extract, mixing until thoroughly combined. Gently stir in the flour mixture, stirring until there are no lumps.

4. **If using mini-donut pans:** Carefully fill each donut indentation ¾ full. Bake for 7–9 minutes or until a toothpick inserted into a donut comes out clean. Transfer donuts to a cooling rack and let cool completely. **If using an electric mini-donut maker:** Carefully fill each donut indentation ¾ full. Bake according to manufacturer's instructions or until a toothpick inserted into a donut comes out clean. Remove donuts from appliance, transfer to a cooling rack, and let cool completely.

5. Place wax paper under a wire rack to collect any drippings for an easy cleanup. Then, in a small saucepan over medium heat, melt butter. Add milk, corn syrup, and chopped chocolate, stirring slowly to allow chocolate to melt completely.

6. Once melted, remove from heat and whisk in powdered sugar. Immediately dip the top of each donut into the icing and transfer to a wire rack.

7. Sprinkle the top of each donut with chopped Whoppers. Let frosting set for 10 minutes and then serve. Donuts can be stored in an airtight container for up to 2 days but are best when eaten fresh.

Chapter 7

DRINKS TO DONUTS

A fruity piña colada, a cold strawberry lemonade, or a creamy glass of rich eggnog. Sometimes you just need a good drink! But why not have your drink and eat it, too . . . in the form of a mini donut? Although the drink-inspired mini donuts in this chapter can't be sipped through a straw, they are the perfect snack when served with their namesake drink. A warm chai tea and a fluffy Chai Tea Mini Donut are the perfect accompaniment to a rainy afternoon. On the other hand, an energizing cup of coffee and a scrumptious Chocolate-Coffee Mini Donut are exactly what you need to start your day with a bang. From happy-hour specials to childhood favorites, you are bound to find your happiness at the bottom of a donut!

Brown Butter–Bourbon Mini Donut

 YIELDS 24 MINI DONUTS

FOR DONUTS

⅔ cup whole milk

2 tablespoons sour cream

1½ cups all-purpose flour, sifted

1½ teaspoons baking powder

¼ teaspoon salt

6 tablespoons browned butter, cooled (see Brown Butter Mini Donut recipe in Chapter 5 to learn how to brown butter)

½ cup granulated sugar

1 large egg

2 teaspoons vanilla extract

1 teaspoon bourbon

FOR ICING

1 tablespoon whole milk

1½ teaspoons vanilla extract

¼ teaspoon bourbon

1½ cups powdered sugar

With the warmth from the bourbon and the nutty flavor from the brown butter, these mini donuts are sure to go down smooth! But be sure to keep this batch away from the kids: It's "adults only" at this mini-donut party!

1. If using an electric donut maker, preheat according to manufacturer's instructions. If using donut pans, preheat oven to 350°F and grease donut pans.
2. In a small bowl, whisk together milk and sour cream. Set aside. In a separate small bowl, whisk together flour, baking powder, and salt. Set aside.
3. In large bowl, cream together cooled browned butter and sugar. Add egg, vanilla extract, and bourbon. Then, alternating flour mixture and milk mixture, combine all ingredients until just blended. Transfer batter to a piping bag, or to a Ziploc bag with the tip cut off.
4. **If using mini-donut pans:** Carefully fill each donut indentation ¾ full. Bake for 7–9 minutes or until a toothpick inserted into a donut comes out clean. Transfer donuts to a cooling rack and cool completely. **If using an electric mini-donut maker:** Carefully fill each donut indentation ¾ full. Bake according to manufacturer's instructions or until a toothpick inserted into a donut comes out clean. Remove donuts from appliance, transfer to a cooling rack, and let cool completely.
5. Place wax paper under a wire rack to collect any drippings for an easy cleanup. Then, in a small bowl, whisk together milk, vanilla extract, bourbon, and powdered sugar until smooth.
6. Dip the top of each donut into the icing, transfer to a wire rack, and let set for 5 minutes. Serve immediately; donuts can be stored in an airtight container for up to 1 day but are best served fresh.

Brown Butter-Bourbon Mini Donut

Chai Tea Mini Donut

 YIELDS 30 MINI DONUTS

FOR DONUTS

1½ teaspoons ground cardamom

1½ teaspoons ground cinnamon

½ teaspoon ground ginger

¼ teaspoon ground cloves

¼ teaspoon ground nutmeg

1⅓ cups all-purpose flour, sifted

2 teaspoons baking powder

¼ teaspoon salt

1 large egg

½ cup granulated sugar

¾ cup whole milk

3 tablespoons vegetable oil

2 teaspoons vanilla extract

FOR ICING

1 tablespoon whole milk

1 teaspoon vanilla extract

1½ cups powdered sugar

Curling up with a cup of your favorite chai tea just got infinitely better with the sweet addition of a Chai Tea Mini Donut. Trade in your fancy tea biscuit for this dense, spicy piece of heaven!

1. If using an electric donut maker, preheat according to manufacturer's instructions. If using donut pans, preheat oven to 350°F and grease donut pans.
2. In a small bowl, whisk together cardamom, cinnamon, ginger, ground cloves, and nutmeg. Remove half of the chai-spice mixture and set aside. Sift the flour, baking powder, and salt into the remaining chai-spice mixture. Set aside.
3. In a medium bowl, whisk together egg and sugar. Then add milk, oil, and vanilla extract, mixing until thoroughly combined. Gently stir in the flour mixture, stirring until there are no lumps.
4. **If using mini-donut pans:** Carefully fill each donut indentation ¾ full. Bake for 7–9 minutes or until a toothpick inserted into a donut comes out clean. Transfer donuts to a cooling rack and cool completely. **If using an electric mini-donut maker:** Carefully fill each donut indentation ¾ full. Bake according to manufacturer's instructions or until a toothpick inserted into a donut comes out clean. Remove donuts from appliance, transfer to a cooling rack, and let cool completely.
5. Place wax paper under a wire rack to collect any drippings for an easy cleanup. Then, in a small bowl, whisk together milk, vanilla extract, powdered sugar, and remaining chai-spice mixture, whisking until smooth.
6. Dip the top of each donut into the icing and transfer to a wire rack and let set for 5 minutes. Serve immediately; donuts can be stored in an airtight container for up to 3 days but are best served fresh.

Cherry Coke Mini Donut

 YIELDS 24 MINI DONUTS

FOR DONUTS

1 cup all-purpose flour, sifted

⅓ cup cocoa powder

2 teaspoons baking powder

¼ teaspoon salt

1 large egg

½ cup granulated sugar

¾ cup Cherry Coke

¼ cup vegetable oil

¼ teaspoon cherry extract

FOR ICING

1½ cups powdered sugar

1½ tablespoons Cherry Coke

Between the bubbly coke and sweet cherry flavor, it's no surprise that Cherry Coke is not a only a hit with the kids, but with the adults too. With a dash of chocolate to deepen the flavor, these Cherry Coke Mini Donuts are a delicious surprise.

1. If using an electric donut maker, preheat according to manufacturer's instructions. If using donut pans, preheat oven to 350°F and grease donut pans.
2. In a small bowl, sift together flour, cocoa powder, baking powder, and salt. Set aside.
3. In a medium bowl, whisk together egg and sugar. Then add Cherry Coke, oil, and cherry extract; mixing until thoroughly combined. Gently stir in the flour mixture, stirring until there are no lumps.
4. **If using mini-donut pans:** Carefully fill each donut indentation ¾ full. Bake for 7–9 minutes or until a toothpick inserted into a donut comes out clean. Transfer donuts to a cooling rack and cool completely. **If using an electric mini-donut maker:** Carefully fill each donut indentation ¾ full. Bake according to manufacturer's instructions or until a toothpick inserted into a donut comes out clean. Remove donuts from appliance, transfer to a cooling rack, and let cool completely.
5. Place wax paper under a wire rack to collect any drippings for an easy cleanup. Then, in a small bowl, whisk together powdered sugar and Cherry Coke until smooth.
6. Dip the top of each donut into the icing, transfer to a wire rack, and let set for 5 minutes. Serve immediately; donuts can be stored in an airtight container for up to 2 days but are best served fresh.

WITH A CHERRY ON TOP

Make this Cherry Coke Mini Donut into a Cherry Coke Float Mini Donut by adding a dollop of whipped cream and a bright red maraschino cherry on top!

Piña Colada Mini Donut

 YIELDS 30 MINI DONUTS

FOR DONUTS

1⅓ cups all-purpose flour, sifted

2 teaspoons baking powder

¼ teaspoon salt

1 large egg

½ cup granulated sugar

½ cup cream of coconut

¼ cup pineapple juice

3 tablespoons vegetable oil

FOR ICING

2 tablespoons cream of coconut

1½ cups powdered sugar

FOR TOPPING

½ cup shredded coconut

24 maraschino cherries

Bartender, please pass a Piña Colada Mini Donut! Swap out that straw for fingers covered in coconut frosting, and dive face-first into these fruity mini donuts that will take you straight to the tropics. You'll feel that warm breeze on your face in no time!

1. If using an electric donut maker, preheat according to manufacturer's instructions. If using donut pans, preheat oven to 350°F and grease donut pans.
2. In a small bowl, sift together flour, baking powder, and salt. Set aside.
3. In a medium bowl, whisk together egg and sugar. Then add cream of coconut, pineapple juice, and oil, mixing until thoroughly combined. Gently stir in the flour mixture, stirring until there are no lumps.
4. **If using mini-donut pans:** Carefully fill each donut indentation ¾ full. Bake for 7–9 minutes or until a toothpick inserted into a donut comes out clean. Transfer donuts to a cooling rack and cool completely. **If using an electric mini-donut maker:** Carefully fill each donut indentation ¾ full. Bake according to manufacturer's instructions or until a toothpick inserted into a donut comes out clean. Remove donuts from appliance, transfer to a cooling rack, and let cool completely.
5. Place wax paper under a wire rack to collect any drippings for an easy cleanup. Then, in a small bowl, whisk together cream of coconut and powdered sugar, whisking until smooth.
6. Dip the top of each donut into the icing and transfer to a wire rack. Sprinkle the tops with shredded coconut, place a maraschino cherry in the center, and let set for 5 minutes. Serve immediately. These donuts do not store well and should be eaten fresh.

Root-Beer Float Mini Donut

 YIELDS 24 MINI DONUTS

FOR DONUTS

1 cup all-purpose flour, sifted

⅓ cup cocoa powder

2 teaspoons baking powder

¼ teaspoon salt

1 large egg

½ cup granulated sugar

¾ cup root beer

¼ cup vegetable oil

FOR ICING

1 cup powdered sugar

1½ tablespoons root beer

FOR WHIPPED CREAM

¾ cup heavy whipping cream

1 teaspoon vanilla extract

3 tablespoons powdered sugar

FOR TOPPING

24 maraschino cherries

Slide up to the counter and order yourself a delicious, creamy root-beer float . . . in mini-donut form! Trade in that big, frosty mug for fingers covered in sweet root-beer glaze and whipped-cream topping. You'll be back for seconds before you know it!

1. If using an electric donut maker, preheat according to manufacturer's instructions. If using donut pans, preheat oven to 350°F and grease donut pans.
2. In a small bowl, sift together flour, cocoa powder, baking powder, and salt. Set aside.
3. In a medium bowl, whisk together egg and sugar. Then add root beer and oil, mixing until thoroughly combined. Gently stir in the flour mixture, stirring until there are no lumps.
4. **If using mini-donut pans:** Carefully fill each donut indentation ¾ full. Bake for 7–9 minutes or until a toothpick inserted into a donut comes out clean. Transfer donuts to a cooling rack and cool completely. **If using an electric mini-donut maker:** Carefully fill each donut indentation ¾ full. Bake according to manufacturer's instructions or until a toothpick inserted into a donut comes out clean. Remove donuts from appliance, transfer to a cooling rack, and let cool completely.
5. Place wax paper under a wire rack to collect any drippings for an easy cleanup. Then, in a small bowl, whisk together powdered sugar and root beer until smooth. Dip the top of each donut into the icing, transfer to a wire rack, and let set for 5 minutes.
6. In a stand mixer, whip cream until peaks are just starting to form. Add vanilla extract and powdered sugar, and continue beating until stiff peaks form. Transfer whipped cream to a piping bag, and pipe onto the tops of the cooled chocolate layer.
7. Top each donut with a maraschino cherry and serve immediately. These donuts do not store well and should be eaten fresh.

Eggnog Mini Donut

Eggnog Mini Donut

 YIELDS 28 MINI DONUTS

FOR DONUTS

1⅓ cups all-purpose flour, sifted

2 teaspoons baking powder

½ teaspoon ground cinnamon

¼ teaspoon nutmeg

¼ teaspoon salt

1 large egg

½ cup granulated sugar

½ cup sour cream

¼ cup vegetable oil

¾ cup eggnog

1 teaspoon vanilla extract

FOR ICING

2 tablespoons eggnog

1 teaspoon vanilla extract

1½ cups powdered sugar

Ah, eggnog! The holiday beverage that is often found clasped in your tipsy aunt's hand as she tells awful stories at all the family holiday parties. But this year, things can be different. Instead, imagine yourself sitting in the corner, eating Eggnog Mini Donuts. It's a much better picture, right?

1. If using an electric donut maker, preheat according to manufacturer's instructions. If using donut pans, preheat oven to 350°F and grease donut pans.
2. In a small bowl, sift together flour, baking powder, cinnamon, nutmeg, and salt. Set aside.
3. In a medium bowl, whisk together egg and sugar. Then add sour cream, oil, and vanilla extract, mixing until thoroughly combined. Gently stir in the flour mixture, alternating with the eggnog, stirring until smooth.
4. **If using mini-donut pans:** Carefully fill each donut indentation ¾ full. Bake for 7–9 minutes or until a toothpick inserted into a donut comes out clean. Transfer donuts to a cooling rack and let cool completely. **If using an electric mini-donut maker:** Carefully fill each donut indentation ¾ full. Bake according to manufacturer's instructions or until a toothpick inserted into a donut comes out clean. Remove donuts from appliance, transfer to a cooling rack, and let cool completely.
5. Place wax paper under a wire rack to collect any drippings for an easy cleanup. Then, in a small bowl, whisk together eggnog and vanilla extract. Add powdered sugar, whisking until smooth.
6. Dip the top of each donut into the icing, transfer to a wire rack, and let set for 5 minutes. Serve immediately; donuts can be stored in an airtight container for up to 3 days but are best served fresh.

FLAVORED EGGNOG

Keep your eyes open around the holidays for some special flavored eggnogs, like Pumpkin-Spice Eggnog and even Sugar-Cookie Eggnog. When baking up a batch of these mini donuts, sub in one of the fun flavored eggnogs for a special twist!

Mimosa Mini Donut

 YIELDS 28 MINI DONUTS

FOR DONUTS

1⅓ cups all-purpose flour, sifted

2 teaspoons baking powder

¼ teaspoon salt

1 large egg

½ cup granulated sugar

Zest of one orange

⅔ cup whole milk

3 tablespoons vegetable oil

1 tablespoon champagne

1 tablespoon orange juice

FOR ICING

1½ cups powdered sugar

1 tablespoon orange juice

1 teaspoon champagne

The mimosa is queen of any brunch party. With the bubbling champagne and the fruity orange juice, mimosas are the perfect breakfast beverage. But rather than just drinking your champagne, try these Mimosa Mini Donuts so you can eat it, too!

1. If using an electric donut maker, preheat according to manufacturer's instructions. If using donut pans, preheat oven to 350°F and grease donut pans.
2. In a small bowl, sift together flour, baking powder, and salt. Set aside.
3. In a medium bowl, whisk together egg, sugar, and orange zest. Then add milk, oil, champagne, and orange juice, mixing until thoroughly combined. Gently stir in the flour mixture, stirring until there are no lumps.
4. **If using mini-donut pans:** Carefully fill each donut indentation ¾ full. Bake for 7–9 minutes or until a toothpick inserted into a donut comes out clean. Transfer donuts to a cooling rack and cool completely. **If using an electric mini-donut maker:** Carefully fill each donut indentation ¾ full. Bake according to manufacturer's instructions or until a toothpick inserted into a donut comes out clean. Remove donuts from appliance, transfer to a cooling rack, and let cool completely.
5. Place wax paper under a wire rack to collect any drippings for an easy cleanup. Then, in a small bowl, whisk together powdered sugar, orange juice, and champagne until smooth.
6. Dip the top of each donut into the icing and transfer to a wire rack and let set for 5 minutes. Serve immediately; donuts can be stored in an airtight container for up to 2 days but are best served fresh.

Chocolate-Coffee Mini Donut

 YIELDS 30 MINI DONUTS

FOR DONUTS

¾ cup whole milk

3 tablespoons vegetable oil

2 teaspoons vanilla extract

2 teaspoons instant espresso granules

1 cup all-purpose flour, sifted

⅓ cup cocoa powder, sifted

2 teaspoons baking powder

¼ teaspoon salt

1 large egg

½ cup granulated sugar

FOR ICING

1½ tablespoons whole milk, warmed

½ teaspoon instant espresso granules

1½ cups powdered sugar

As any good coffee drinker knows, creamy chocolate and stout coffee are the perfect partners. The chocolate flavor in this tender donut is intensified by the espresso, but the espresso stands out in the icing!

1. If using an electric donut maker, preheat according to manufacturer's instructions. If using donut pans, preheat oven to 350°F and grease donut pans.

2. In a small bowl, whisk together milk, oil, vanilla extract, and instant espresso granules. Set aside. In a small bowl, sift together flour, cocoa powder, baking powder, and salt. Set aside.

3. In a medium bowl, whisk together egg and sugar. Then add milk mixture, mixing until thoroughly combined. Gently stir in the flour mixture, stirring until there are no lumps.

4. **If using mini-donut pans:** Carefully fill each donut indentation ¾ full. Bake for 7–9 minutes or until a toothpick inserted into a donut comes out clean. Transfer donuts to a cooling rack and cool completely. **If using an electric mini-donut maker:** Carefully fill each donut indentation ¾ full. Bake according to manufacturer's instructions or until a toothpick inserted into a donut comes out clean. Remove donuts from appliance, transfer to a cooling rack, and let cool completely.

5. Place wax paper under a wire rack to collect any drippings for an easy cleanup. Then, in a small bowl, whisk together warm milk and instant espresso granules, stirring until dissolved. Add powdered sugar, whisking until smooth.

6. Dip the top of each donut into the icing, transfer to a wire rack, and let set for 5 minutes. Serve immediately; donuts can be stored in an airtight container for up to 3 days but are best served fresh.

Almond-Brandy Mini Donut

 YIELDS 24 MINI DONUTS

Since most donuts are made with vanilla, mixing almond extract and brandy is a fun, fresh way to surprise your taste buds. But keep this batch away from the kids. This after-dinner mini donut is adults-only!

FOR DONUTS

⅔ cup whole milk

2 tablespoons sour cream

1½ cups all-purpose flour, sifted

1½ teaspoons baking powder

¼ teaspoon salt

6 tablespoons butter, room temperature

½ cup granulated sugar

1 large egg

2 teaspoons almond extract

1 teaspoon brandy

FOR ICING

1 tablespoon whole milk

1½ teaspoons almond extract

¼ teaspoon brandy

1½ cups powdered sugar

1. If using an electric donut maker, preheat according to manufacturer's instructions. If using donut pans, preheat oven to 350°F and grease donut pans.

2. In a small bowl, whisk together milk and sour cream. Set aside. In a separate small bowl, whisk together flour, baking powder, and salt. Set aside.

3. In a large bowl or a stand mixer, cream together butter and sugar until light and fluffy—about 1 minute. Add egg, almond extract, and brandy. Beat for 30 seconds, scraping down the bowl as needed.

4. Then, alternating flour mixture and milk mixture, combine all ingredients until just blended. Transfer batter to a piping bag, or to a Ziploc bag with the tip cut off.

5. **If using mini-donut pans:** Carefully fill each donut indentation ¾ full. Bake for 7–9 minutes or until a toothpick inserted into a donut comes out clean. Transfer donuts to a cooling rack and cool completely. **If using an electric mini-donut maker:** Carefully fill each donut indentation ¾ full. Bake according to manufacturer's instructions or until a toothpick inserted into a donut comes out clean. Remove donuts from appliance, transfer to a cooling rack, and let cool completely.

6. Place wax paper under a wire rack to collect any drippings for an easy cleanup. Then, in a small bowl, whisk together milk, almond extract, brandy, and powdered sugar, until smooth.

7. Dip the top of each donut into the icing, transfer to a wire rack, and let set for 5 minutes. Serve immediately; donuts can be stored in an airtight container for up to 1 day but are best served fresh.

Dr Pepper Fried Mini Donut

 YIELDS 16 MINI DONUTS

FOR DONUTS

1 cup all-purpose flour

1½ teaspoons baking powder

½ teaspoon salt

1 large egg

⅓ cup granulated sugar

1 teaspoon vanilla extract

⅓ cup Dr Pepper

Vegetable oil or peanut oil, for frying

FOR ICING

1½ cups powdered sugar

1½ tablespoons Dr Pepper

Dr Pepper gives these mini donuts a wonderful, light texture and a scrumptious flavor. With just a few quick whisks, you will be dropping batter into the oil in no time! Easy, fast, and tasty, these mini donuts might turn out to be your favorite!

1. Heat oil in a large, deep skillet or a deep fryer to 350°F.
2. In a small bowl, sift together flour, baking powder, and salt. Set aside.
3. In a medium bowl, whisk together egg and sugar. Then add vanilla extract and Dr Pepper, mixing until thoroughly combined. Gently stir in the flour mixture, stirring until there are no lumps.
4. Once oil is hot, working with 4 to 6 donuts at a time, carefully drop rounded tablespoons of dough into oil. Fry for 1–2 minutes or until golden brown; flip each donut and fry the other side.
5. Remove and drain on a plate lined with newspaper or paper towels. Continue this process until each donut has been fried.
6. Place wax paper under a wire rack to collect any drippings for an easy cleanup. Then, in a small bowl, whisk together powdered sugar and Dr Pepper until smooth.
7. While still warm, dip the tops of donuts into the icing, transfer to a wire rack, and let set for 2 minutes. Serve immediately; donuts can be stored in an airtight container for up to 3 days but are best served fresh.

Peppermint-Mocha Mini Donut

 YIELDS 30 MINI DONUTS

FOR DONUTS

1 cup all-purpose flour, sifted

¼ cup chocolate malted-milk powder, sifted

1 tablespoon cocoa powder, sifted

2 teaspoons baking powder

¼ teaspoon salt

1 large egg

½ cup granulated sugar

¾ cup whole milk

3 tablespoons vegetable oil

1 teaspoon vanilla extract

FOR CHOCOLATE ICING

4 tablespoons butter

2 tablespoons whole milk

1 tablespoon light corn syrup

2 ounces bittersweet chocolate, roughly chopped

1 cup powdered sugar, sifted

FOR WHIPPED CREAM

¾ cup heavy whipping cream

½ teaspoon vanilla extract

3 tablespoons powdered sugar

FOR TOPPING

⅓ cup finely crushed peppermints

With their mint and cream combination, peppermint mochas have been a coffeehouse delicacy for years. By fusing these flavors into a mini donut, the peppermint mocha takes on a whole new level of awesome!

1. If using an electric donut maker, preheat according to manufacturer's instructions. If using donut pans, preheat oven to 350°F and grease donut pans.
2. In a small bowl, sift together flour, malted-milk powder, cocoa powder, baking powder, and salt. Set aside.
3. In a medium bowl, whisk together egg and sugar. Then add milk, oil, and vanilla extract, mixing until thoroughly combined. Gently stir in the flour mixture, stirring until there are no lumps.
4. **If using mini-donut pans:** Carefully fill each donut indentation ¾ full. Bake for 7–9 minutes or until a toothpick inserted into a donut comes out clean. Transfer donuts to a cooling rack and let cool completely. **If using an electric mini-donut maker:** Carefully fill each donut indentation ¾ full. Bake according to manufacturer's instructions or until a toothpick inserted into a donut comes out clean. Remove donuts from appliance, transfer to a cooling rack, and let cool completely.
5. Place wax paper under a wire rack to collect any drippings for an easy cleanup. Then, in a small saucepan over medium heat, melt butter. Add milk, corn syrup, and chopped chocolate, stirring slowly to allow chocolate to melt completely.
6. Once melted, remove from heat and whisk in powdered sugar. Immediately dip the top of each donut into the icing and transfer to a wire rack. Let cool for 10 minutes.
7. In a stand mixer, whip cream until peaks are just starting to form. Add powdered sugar and vanilla extract, and continue beating until stiff peaks form. Transfer whipped cream to a piping bag, and pipe onto the tops of the cooled chocolate layer.
8. Sprinkle the top of each donut with chopped peppermints and serve immediately. These donuts do not store well and so should be eaten fresh.

Peppermint-Mocha Mini Donuts

Strawberry Lemonade Mini Donut

 YIELDS 24 MINI DONUTS

FOR DONUTS

⅔ cup whole milk

2 tablespoons sour cream

1½ cups all-purpose flour, sifted

1½ teaspoons baking powder

¼ teaspoon salt

6 tablespoons butter, room temperature

½ cup granulated sugar

1 large egg

Zest of 1 large lemon

2 tablespoons lemon juice

FOR ICING

1 tablespoon whole milk

2 teaspoons strawberry extract

3–4 drops red food coloring

1½ cups powdered sugar

This refreshing summertime drink made with zesty lemons and bountiful strawberries makes a spectacular mini donut. Between the zesty lemon cake donut and fruity strawberry pink icing, these little darlings are sure to be a new favorite.

1. If using an electric donut maker, preheat according to manufacturer's instructions. If using donut pans, preheat oven to 350°F and grease donut pans.
2. In a small bowl, whisk together milk and sour cream. Set aside. In a separate small bowl, whisk together flour, baking powder, and salt. Set aside.
3. In a large bowl or a stand mixer, cream together butter and sugar until light and fluffy—about 1 minute. Add egg, lemon zest, and lemon juice. Beat for 30 seconds, scraping down the bowl as needed.
4. Then, alternating flour mixture and milk mixture, combine all ingredients until just blended. Transfer batter to a piping bag, or to a Ziploc bag with the tip cut off.
5. **If using mini-donut pans:** Carefully fill each donut indentation ¾ full. Bake for 7–9 minutes or until a toothpick inserted into a donut comes out clean. Transfer donuts to a cooling rack and cool completely. **If using an electric mini-donut maker:** Carefully fill each donut indentation ¾ full. Bake according to manufacturer's instructions or until a toothpick inserted into a donut comes out clean. Remove donuts from appliance, transfer to a cooling rack, and let cool completely.
6. Place wax paper under a wire rack to collect any drippings for an easy cleanup. Then, in a small bowl, whisk together milk, strawberry extract, and red food coloring. Add powdered sugar, whisking until smooth.
7. Dip the top of each donut into the icing, transfer to a wire rack, and let set for 5 minutes. Serve immediately, or store in an airtight container for up to 3 days.

Irish Coffee Mini Donut

 YIELDS 30 MINI DONUTS

FOR DONUTS

¾ cup whole milk

3 tablespoons vegetable oil

2 teaspoons vanilla extract

2 teaspoons instant espresso granules

1⅓ cups all-purpose flour, sifted

2 teaspoons baking powder

¼ teaspoon salt

1 large egg

½ cup granulated sugar

FOR ICING

1½ tablespoons Baileys Irish Cream

1½ cups powdered sugar

In this recipe, dark espresso and smooth Baileys Irish Cream come together to create a spectacular Irish Coffee Mini Donut. The combination is delicious, smooth, and perfect for an adult brunch for St. Paddy's Day!

1. If using an electric donut maker, preheat according to manufacturer's instructions. If using donut pans, preheat oven to 350°F and grease donut pans.
2. In a small bowl, whisk together milk, oil, vanilla extract, and instant espresso granules. Set aside. In a small bowl, sift together flour, baking powder, and salt. Set aside.
3. In a medium bowl, whisk together egg and sugar. Then add milk mixture, mixing until thoroughly combined. Gently stir in the flour mixture, stirring until there are no lumps.
4. **If using mini-donut pans:** Carefully fill each donut indentation ¾ full. Bake for 7–9 minutes or until a toothpick inserted into a donut comes out clean. Transfer donuts to a cooling rack and cool completely. **If using an electric mini-donut maker:** Carefully fill each donut indentation ¾ full. Bake according to manufacturer's instructions or until a toothpick inserted into a donut comes out clean. Remove donuts from appliance, transfer to a cooling rack, and let cool completely.
5. Place wax paper under a wire rack to collect any drippings for an easy cleanup. Then, in a small bowl, whisk together Baileys Irish Cream and powdered sugar, whisking until smooth.
6. Dip the top of each donut into the icing, transfer to a wire rack, and let set for 5 minutes. Serve immediately; donuts can be stored in an airtight container for up to 3 days but are best served fresh.

Guinness-Dark Chocolate Glazed Mini Donut

 YIELDS 24 MINI DONUTS

FOR DONUTS

1 cup all-purpose flour, sifted

⅓ cup cocoa powder

2 teaspoons baking powder

¼ teaspoon salt

1 large egg

½ cup granulated sugar

¾ cup Guinness beer

¼ cup vegetable oil

FOR ICING

1½ cups powdered sugar

1½ tablespoons whole milk

1 teaspoon vanilla extract

Of all the types of beer, a stout like Guinness is the perfect accompaniment to a chocolate donut. With the delicious notes of chocolate and coffee throughout the stout, you don't need as much cocoa powder to get that dark chocolate flavor you crave!

1. If using an electric donut maker, preheat according to manufacturer's instructions. If using donut pans, preheat oven to 350°F and grease donut pans.
2. In a small bowl, sift together flour, cocoa powder, baking powder, and salt. Set aside.
3. In a medium bowl, whisk together egg and sugar. Then add Guinness beer and oil, mixing until thoroughly combined. Gently stir in the flour mixture, stirring until there are no lumps.
4. **If using mini-donut pans:** Carefully fill each donut indentation ¾ full. Bake for 7–9 minutes or until a toothpick inserted into a donut comes out clean. Transfer donuts to a cooling rack and cool completely. **If using an electric mini-donut maker:** Carefully fill each donut indentation ¾ full. Bake according to manufacturer's instructions or until a toothpick inserted into a donut comes out clean. Remove donuts from appliance, transfer to a cooling rack, and let cool completely.
5. Place wax paper under a wire rack to collect any drippings for an easy cleanup. Then, in a small bowl, whisk together powdered sugar, milk, and vanilla extract until smooth.
6. Dip the top of each donut into the icing, transfer to a wire rack, and let set for 5 minutes. Serve immediately; donuts can be stored in an airtight container for up to 3 days but are best served fresh.

Chapter 8

FOR THE KID IN YOU

Do you remember enjoying peanut butter and jelly sandwiches during snack time on the playground? Were you the kid stuffing your face with Cap'n Crunch cereal at the crack of dawn on Saturday mornings? Or how about making delicious s'mores around the campfire on cold nights? In this chapter, childhood nostalgia is being served up on a platter in adorable mini-donut form. Here, you'll find fun recipes like Caramel-Apple Fritters, a flavorful apple donut with a sticky, sweet caramel glaze; a tasty Butterscotch Mini Donut that will instantly transport you back to Grandma's house and her bowlful of candies; and a mini donut made for a party in the Confetti Cake Mini Donut. With these soon-to-be favorites, you can say goodbye to the days when you felt "too grown up" for Fluffernutter sandwiches or confetti cakes, because these recipes are totally for the kid in you!

Cookies and Cream Mini Donuts

Cookies and Cream Mini Donut

 YIELDS 28 MINI DONUTS

FOR DONUTS

1⅓ cups all-purpose flour, sifted

½ cup cocoa powder

2 teaspoons baking powder

¼ teaspoon salt

1 large egg

¾ cup granulated sugar

3 tablespoons vegetable oil

¼ cup sour cream

1 teaspoon vanilla extract

½ cup whole milk

FOR ICING

1½ tablespoons heavy cream

1 teaspoon vanilla extract

1½ cups powdered sugar

FOR TOPPING

½ cup chopped Oreo cookies

How do you eat your Oreos? Do you twist and eat the cream first, or do you dunk them into a cold glass of milk? How about trying them chopped up on top of a chocolate cake donut with a delicious cream frosting? Why not? It's the best of both worlds!

1. If using an electric donut maker, preheat according to manufacturer's instructions. If using donut pans, preheat oven to 350°F and grease donut pans.
2. In a small bowl, sift together flour, cocoa powder, baking powder, and salt. Set aside.
3. In a medium bowl, whisk together egg and sugar. Then add oil, sour cream, and vanilla extract, mixing until thoroughly combined. Gently stir in the flour mixture, alternating with the milk, stirring until there are no lumps.
4. **If using mini-donut pans:** Carefully fill each donut indentation ¾ full. Bake for 7–9 minutes or until a toothpick inserted into a donut comes out clean. Transfer donuts to a cooling rack and cool completely. **If using an electric mini-donut maker:** Carefully fill each donut indentation ¾ full. Bake according to manufacturer's instructions or until a toothpick inserted into a donut comes out clean. Remove donuts from appliance, transfer to a cooling rack, and let cool 5 minutes.
5. Place wax paper under a wire rack to collect any drippings for an easy cleanup. Then, in a small bowl, whisk together heavy cream and vanilla extract. Add powdered sugar and whisk until smooth.
6. Dip the top of each donut into the icing and transfer to a wire rack. Sprinkle the top of each donut with chopped Oreo cookies and let set for 5 minutes. Serve immediately, or store in an airtight container in the refrigerator for up to 2 days.

Confetti Cake Mini Donut

 YIELDS 30 MINI DONUTS

FOR DONUTS

1⅓ cups all-purpose flour, sifted

2 teaspoons baking powder

¼ teaspoon salt

1 large egg

½ cup granulated sugar

¾ cup whole milk

3 tablespoons vegetable oil

2 teaspoons vanilla extract

2.5 ounces multicolored sprinkles

FOR ICING

1 tablespoon whole milk

1 teaspoon vanilla extract

1½ cups powdered sugar

These donuts scream party . . . at least they would if donuts could talk. From the outside, you can see little specks of color, but the big surprise is on the inside. Brightly colored explosions fill each bite, making these mini donuts the perfect birthday breakfast!

1. If using an electric donut maker, preheat according to manufacturer's instructions. If using donut pans, preheat oven to 350°F and grease donut pans.
2. In a small bowl, sift together flour, baking powder, and salt. Set aside.
3. In a medium bowl, whisk together egg and sugar. Then add milk, oil, and vanilla extract, mixing until thoroughly combined. Gently stir in the flour mixture and the sprinkles, stirring until there are no lumps.
4. **If using mini-donut pans:** Carefully fill each donut indentation ¾ full. Bake for 7–9 minutes or until a toothpick inserted into a donut comes out clean. Transfer donuts to a cooling rack and cool completely. **If using an electric mini-donut maker:** Carefully fill each donut indentation ¾ full. Bake according to manufacturer's instructions or until a toothpick inserted into a donut comes out clean. Remove donuts from appliance, transfer to a cooling rack, and let cool completely.
5. Place wax paper under a wire rack to collect any drippings for an easy cleanup. Then, in a small bowl, whisk together milk and vanilla extract. Add powdered sugar, whisking until smooth.
6. Dip the top of each donut into the icing, transfer to a wire rack, and let set for 5 minutes. Serve immediately; donuts can be stored in an airtight container for up to 3 days but are best served fresh.

Confetti Cake Mini Donuts

Fluffernutter Mini Donuts

 YIELDS 30 MINI DONUTS

FOR DONUTS

1 cup all-purpose flour

2 teaspoons baking powder

¼ teaspoon salt

½ cup granulated sugar

¼ cup creamy peanut butter

1 large egg

¾ cup whole milk

2 tablespoons vegetable oil

FOR FROSTING

½ cup Marshmallow Fluff

When these peanut butter donuts are smeared with clouds of Marshmallow Fluff, they bring back a flood of childhood memories of sticky fingers and Fluffernutter sandwiches. Serve with a cold glass of milk to really up the nostalgia factor!

1. If using an electric donut maker, preheat according to manufacturer's instructions. If using donut pans, preheat oven to 350°F and grease donut pans.
2. In a small bowl, whisk together flour, baking powder, and salt. Set aside.
3. In a medium bowl, cream together sugar and peanut butter until light and fluffy. Then add egg, milk, and oil, mixing until thoroughly combined. Then, alternating the flour mixture and milk mixture, combine all ingredients until there are no lumps.
4. **If using mini-donut pans:** Carefully fill each donut indentation ¾ full. Bake for 6–8 minutes or until donuts are slightly browned and spring back when touched. Remove from oven, transfer to a cooling rack, and cool for 5 minutes. **If using an electric mini-donut maker:** Carefully fill each donut indentation ¾ full. Bake according to manufacturer's instructions or until the donuts are slightly browned and spring back when touched. Transfer donuts to a cooling rack and cool for 5 minutes.
5. While the donuts are still warm to the touch, frost the tops with a healthy smear of Marshmallow Fluff. These donuts are best served while still warm, so serve immediately.

FLUFFERNUTTER 101

The Fluffernutter sandwich is two slices of white bread, slathered with peanut butter and Marshmallow Fluff. It has been a childhood favorite since the early 1900s and originated in the northeastern United States.

PB&J Mini Donut

 YIELDS 30 MINI DONUTS

Peanut butter and jelly sandwiches have been a childhood favorite forever. But you don't have to give up these flavors just because you're a grownup. With the tastes of creamy peanut butter and sweet jelly, these mini donuts are sure to take you back!

FOR DONUTS

1 cup all-purpose flour

2 teaspoons baking powder

¼ teaspoon salt

½ cup granulated sugar

¼ cup creamy peanut butter

1 large egg

¾ cup whole milk

2 tablespoons vegetable oil

FOR FILLING

⅓ cup strawberry jelly

FOR ICING

1 tablespoon whole milk

2 teaspoons strawberry extract

3–4 drops red food coloring

1½ cups powdered sugar

1. If using an electric donut maker, preheat according to manufacturer's instructions. If using donut pans, preheat oven to 350°F and grease donut pans.
2. In a small bowl, whisk together flour, baking powder, and salt. Set aside.
3. In a medium bowl, cream together sugar and peanut butter until light and fluffy. Then add egg, milk, and oil, mixing until thoroughly combined. Then, alternating the flour mixture and milk mixture, combine all ingredients until there are no lumps.
4. Transfer batter to a piping bag, or a Ziploc bag with the tip cut off. Also place strawberry jelly in a piping bag, or to a Ziploc bag with the tip cut off for easier use.
5. **If using mini-donut pans:** Carefully fill each donut indentation ¾ full with donut batter. Then, pipe in a circle of strawberry jelly. Bake for 6–8 minutes or until donuts are slightly browned and spring back when touched. Remove from oven, transfer to a cooling rack, and cool for 5 minutes. **If using an electric mini-donut maker:** Carefully fill each donut indentation ¾ full with donut batter. Then, pipe in a circle of strawberry jelly. Bake according to manufacturer's instructions or until donuts are slightly browned and spring back when touched. Transfer donuts to a cooling rack and cool for 5 minutes.
6. Place wax paper under a wire rack to collect any drippings for an easy cleanup. Then, in a small bowl, whisk together milk, strawberry extract, and red food coloring. Add powdered sugar, whisking until smooth.
7. Dip the top of each donut into the icing, transfer to a wire rack, and let set for 5 minutes. Serve immediately, or store in an airtight container for up to 2 days.

GRAPE IT UP

To change up the flavors on this mini donut, all you have to do is switch out the jelly flavors. Instead of strawberry, try classic grape, peach, or even red plum. The flavor choices are endless!

S'mores Mini Donut

 YIELDS 30 MINI DONUTS

FOR DONUTS

1 cup all-purpose flour, sifted

⅓ cup cocoa powder, sifted

2 teaspoons baking powder

¼ teaspoon salt

1 large egg

½ cup granulated sugar

¾ cup whole milk

2 tablespoons vegetable oil

2 tablespoons sour cream

½ teaspoon vanilla extract

FOR TOPPING

½ cup Marshmallow Fluff

3 graham crackers, crushed

2 ounces milk chocolate, chopped

Everyone remembers sitting around the campfire, grilling marshmallows, and making unbelievably delicious s'mores. These sweet treats are a true American classic. Whether they are found around a campfire or in mini-donut form, the mix of chocolate, graham crackers, and marshmallows is always a hit!

1. If using an electric donut maker, preheat according to manufacturer's instructions. If using donut pans, preheat oven to 350°F and grease donut pans.
2. In a small bowl, sift together flour, cocoa powder, baking powder, and salt. Set aside.
3. In a medium bowl, whisk together egg and sugar. Then add milk, oil, sour cream, and vanilla extract, mixing until thoroughly combined. Gently stir in the flour mixture, stirring until there are no lumps.
4. **If using mini-donut pans:** Carefully fill each donut indentation ¾ full. Bake for 7–9 minutes or until a toothpick inserted into a donut comes out clean. Transfer donuts to a cooling rack and let cool completely. **If using an electric mini-donut maker:** Carefully fill each donut indentation ¾ full. Bake according to manufacturer's instructions or until a toothpick inserted into a donut comes out clean. Remove donuts from appliance, transfer to a cooling rack, and let cool completely.
5. Generously spread the top of each donut with Marshmallow Fluff, and then dip into the crushed graham crackers. Then, in a small, microwave-safe bowl, melt milk chocolate and drizzle over the top of each donut.
6. Let chocolate set for 1 minute and then serve. These donuts do not store well when assembled. Store donut (without toppings) in an airtight container for up to 2 days and then assemble before serving.

TORCH IT, BABY!

If you have a kitchen torch, swap out the Marshmallow Fluff for mini marshmallows and give these S'mores Mini Donuts more of a campfire feel. Just quickly torch the tops of the mini marsh-mallows for a few seconds or until they are slightly browned, and then . . . dig in!

S'mores Mini Donuts

Hot Chocolate Mini Donuts

Hot Chocolate Mini Donut

 YIELDS 30 MINI DONUTS

FOR DONUTS

1 cup all-purpose flour, sifted

¼ cup powdered hot chocolate mix (approximately 1½ packages)

2 tablespoons cocoa powder, sifted

2 teaspoons baking powder

¼ teaspoon salt

1 large egg

½ cup granulated sugar

¾ cup whole milk

2 tablespoons vegetable oil

2 tablespoons sour cream

½ teaspoon vanilla extract

FOR ICING

4 tablespoons butter

2 tablespoons whole milk

1 tablespoon light corn syrup

2 ounces bittersweet chocolate, roughly chopped

1 cup powdered sugar, sifted

FOR TOPPING

½ cup mini marshmallows

MEXICAN HOT CHOCOLATE

Traditional Mexican hot chocolate is made using a bar of Mexican chocolate, milk, cinnamon, and vanilla. For a fun variation on this recipe, add in ½ teaspoon ground cinnamon and a pinch of chili powder to make Mexican Hot Chocolate Mini Donuts.

Between the sweet chocolate donut, rich chocolate frosting, and creamy mini marshmallows, these Hot Chocolate Mini Donuts are the prefect replica of a mug of hot chocolate. Hot chocolate has been warming up cold nights for centuries, and now you can warm yourself up with these mini donuts anytime you get a chill!

1. If using an electric donut maker, preheat according to manufacturer's instructions. If using donut pans, preheat oven to 350°F and grease donut pans.
2. In a small bowl, sift together flour, hot chocolate mix, cocoa powder, baking powder, and salt. Set aside.
3. In a medium bowl, whisk together egg and sugar. Then add milk, oil, sour cream, and vanilla extract, mixing until thoroughly combined. Gently stir in the flour mixture, stirring until there are no lumps.
4. **If using mini-donut pans:** Carefully fill each donut indentation ¾ full. Bake for 7–9 minutes or until a toothpick inserted into a donut comes out clean. Transfer donuts to a cooling rack and let cool completely. **If using an electric mini-donut maker:** Carefully fill each donut indentation ¾ full. Bake according to manufacturer's instructions or until a toothpick inserted into a donut comes out clean. Remove donuts from appliance, transfer to a cooling rack, and let cool completely.
5. Place wax paper under a wire rack to collect any drippings for an easy cleanup. Then, in a small saucepan over medium heat, melt butter. Add milk, corn syrup, and chopped chocolate, stirring slowly to allow chocolate to melt completely.
6. Once melted, remove from heat and whisk in powdered sugar. Immediately dip the top of each donut into the icing and transfer to a wire rack.
7. Top each donut with mini marshmallows. Let frosting set for 10 minutes and then serve. Donuts can be stored in an airtight container for up to 2 days but are best when eaten fresh.

Caramel-Apple Fritter

FOR FRITTERS

1 cup all-purpose flour

1½ teaspoons baking powder

1 teaspoon cinnamon

½ teaspoon salt

¼ teaspoon nutmeg

1 large egg

⅓ cup granulated sugar

½ teaspoon vanilla extract

⅓ cup whole milk

1 heaping cup peeled and chopped apple

Vegetable oil or peanut oil, for frying

FOR CARAMEL SAUCE

16 caramel squares, unwrapped

2 teaspoons whole milk

With their bright colors and sweet-tart flavors, caramel apples have always been a favorite fall treat. In celebration of these deliciously sweet apples, in this recipe you'll find a scrumptious apple fritter dipped in a sticky caramel sauce. Amazing!

1. Heat oil in a large, deep skillet or a deep fryer to 350°F.
2. In a small bowl, sift together flour, baking powder, cinnamon, salt, and nutmeg. Set aside.
3. In a medium bowl, whisk together egg and sugar. Then add vanilla extract and milk, mixing until thoroughly combined. Gently stir in the flour mixture, stirring until there are no lumps. Gently fold in chopped apple.
4. Once oil is hot, working with 4 to 6 fritters at a time, carefully drop into dough by rounded tablespoons into oil. Fry for 1–2 minutes or until golden brown; flip each donut and fry the other side.
5. Remove and drain on a plate lined with newspaper or paper towels. Continue this process until each fritter has been fried.
6. Place wax paper under a wire rack to collect any drippings for an easy cleanup. In a small microwave-safe bowl, place caramel squares and milk. Microwave on high, stirring every 15 seconds, until smooth.
7. While still warm, dip the top of each fritter into the caramel and transfer to a wire rack. These fritters do not store well, so serve immediately.

Rainbow Glaze Mini Donut

 YIELDS 30 MINI DONUTS

FOR DONUTS

1⅓ cups all-purpose flour, sifted

2 teaspoons baking powder

¼ teaspoon salt

1 large egg

½ cup granulated sugar

¾ cup whole milk

3 tablespoons vegetable oil

2 teaspoons vanilla extract

2–3 drops of 4 different food colorings of your choice

FOR ICING

1 tablespoon whole milk

1 teaspoon vanilla extract

1½ cups powdered sugar

Are you craving a traditionally flavored donut, but want to make one with a fun surprise on the inside? Then these Rainbow Glaze Mini Donuts are the ones for you! While the outside of this donut looks light brown, once you crack it open, you are treated to bright swirls of color that are guaranteed to make you smile!

1. If using an electric donut maker, preheat according to manufacturer's instructions. If using donut pans, preheat oven to 350°F and grease donut pans.
2. In a small bowl, sift together flour, baking powder, and salt. Set aside.
3. In a medium bowl, whisk together egg and sugar. Then add milk, oil, and vanilla extract, mixing until thoroughly combined. Gently stir in the flour mixture, stirring until there are no lumps.
4. Divide batter between five small bowls. Leaving one bowl white, color the other four bowls of batter with your choice of food coloring. Then, into a piping bag, or into a Ziploc bag with the tip cut off, spoon 2 tablespoons of each batter. Repeat process until there is no batter remaining.
5. **If using mini-donut pans:** Carefully fill each donut indentation ¾ full. Bake for 7–9 minutes or until a toothpick inserted into a donut comes out clean. Transfer donuts to a cooling rack and cool completely. **If using an electric mini-donut maker:** Carefully fill each donut indentation ¾ full. Bake according to manufacturer's instructions or until a toothpick inserted into a donut comes out clean. Remove donuts from appliance, transfer to a cooling rack, and let cool completely.
6. Place wax paper under a wire rack to collect any drippings for an easy cleanup. Then, in a small bowl, whisk together milk and vanilla extract. Add powdered sugar, whisking until smooth.
7. Dip the top of each donut into the icing, transfer to a wire rack, and let set for 5 minutes. Serve immediately, or store in an airtight container for up to 3 days.

Butterscotch Mini Donut

 YIELDS 30 MINI DONUTS

FOR DONUTS

1⅓ cups all-purpose flour, sifted

2 teaspoons baking powder

½ teaspoon cinnamon

¼ teaspoon salt

1 large egg

½ cup granulated sugar

¾ cup whole milk

3 tablespoons vegetable oil

2 teaspoons vanilla extract

FOR ICING

¾ cup butterscotch morsels

1 tablespoon whole milk

While butterscotch may bring back images of your grandmother's house and her bowl of hard candy, these aren't your grandmother's donuts. With a pinch of cinnamon thrown into the batter, and a creamy butterscotch icing, these Butterscotch Mini Donuts are little bites of heaven that are as modern as you are!

1. If using an electric donut maker, preheat according to manufacturer's instructions. If using donut pans, preheat oven to 350°F and grease donut pans.
2. In a small bowl, sift together flour, baking powder, cinnamon, and salt. Set aside.
3. In a medium bowl, whisk together egg and sugar. Then add milk, oil, and vanilla extract, mixing until thoroughly combined. Gently stir in the flour mixture, stirring until there are no lumps.
4. **If using mini-donut pans:** Carefully fill each donut indentation ¾ full. Bake for 7–9 minutes or until a toothpick inserted into a donut comes out clean. Transfer donuts to a cooling rack and cool completely. **If using an electric mini-donut maker:** Carefully fill each donut indentation ¾ full. Bake according to manufacturer's instructions or until a toothpick inserted into a donut comes out clean. Remove donuts from appliance and transfer to a cooling rack and cool completely.
5. Place wax paper under a wire rack to collect any drippings for an easy cleanup. Then, in a small, microwave-safe bowl, microwave the butterscotch morsels and milk in 15-second increments, stirring each time. Once you reach a smooth, lump-free butterscotch glaze, let it cool for 2 minutes.
6. Dip the top of each donut into the icing, transfer to a wire rack, and let set for 5 minutes. Serve immediately, or store in an airtight container for up to 3 days.

Butterscotch Mini Donuts

INDEX

Note: Page numbers in *italics* indicate photographs.

A

B

About the Author

Jessica Segarra is the author-baker-cook-photographer behind *The Novice Chef* blog (*www.thenovicechefblog.com*). She grew up in the kitchen, sandwiched between her grandmother, who specializes in true Cajun gumbo; and her mother, who eats frosting with a giant spoon. Jessica has hosted cooking segments on *Good Morning Jacksonville* and for *Costco/Pork Be Inspired!* She has developed recipes for brand-name companies like Betty Crocker, Kraft, Chobani, Kerrygold, and Wasa. *The Novice Chef* blog has been taking over the Internet since December 2008 and has been featured on websites like Gizmodo, The Kitchn, and more. She's also appeared in *Shape* magazine, *Parenting* magazine, and on The Cooking Channel. Jessica currently lives in Jacksonville, Florida, with her husband Jorge and five rescue pets.